Macramé
FOR BEGINNERS

A Complete Step-By-Step Illustrated Guide For Adult Beginners To Realize Amazing Knitted Projects. Master the Best Macramé Techniques And Turn it into a Profitable Business

Benedikta Weber

Copyright 2022 by Benedikta Weber

All rights reserved. This book or any portion thereof may not be reproduced or used in any manner whatsoever, mechanical, photocopying, photographic, any form of recording, or electronic process, nor stored in any retrieval system, transmitted, or otherwise copied for public or private use, without the express written permission of the author except for the fair use as brief quotations embodied in articles and printed reviews.

Table of Contents

Introduction — 07

Chapter 1 - The Origins of Macramé — 08

What is Macramé — 10
History of Macramé — 12
How to Get Started with Macramé — 13
Is Macramé Really Difficult to Learn? — 14

Chapter 2 - Different Tools and Materials — 16

Yarn — 16
Scissors — 17
Measuring Tools — 18
Cords — 20
Embroidery Needles — 21
Clothes Rail — 22

Chapter 3 - Knots and Techniques — 24

Supplies and Materials — 24
Lark's Head Knot — 25
Reverse Lark's Head Knot — 26
Square Knots and Half Knots — 27
Spiral Stitch — 29
Clove Hitch — 30
Overhand Knot — 31
Gathering Knot — 32
Wrapping Knot — 33

Half Hitch	34
Cow Hitch Knot	35
Barrel Knot	36
Constrictor Knot	37
Josephine Knot	38
Chinese Crown Knot	39

Chapter 4 - Things to Avoid in Macramé   41

5 Mistakes to Avoid in Macramé as a Beginner	41
Some Common Macramé Errors and their Troubleshooting	44

Chapter 5 - Macramé Projects   46

For the Home

• Wall Hanging	47
• Macramé Dream Catcher	63
• Easy Wall Hanging	75
• Macramé Chandelier	77
• Pillow Cover	87

For Planters

• Plant Hanger	92

For the Holidays (Christmas, Halloween)

• Feather Ornament	96
• Boho Ornament	102
• Christmas Wreath	110
• Halloween Pumpkin Cover	118

For Accessories

• Mason Jars	131
• Macramé Placemat	136
• Macramé Banner	139
• Macramé Garland	141

Chapter 6 - Turn this Hobby into a Side Hustle — 144

Sell your Macramé pieces to friends and family — 144
Sell your Macramé Pieces at local Craft Fairs — 145
Become a local wholesaler — 146
Give local workshops — 147
Start a YouTube channel — 148
Sell your Macramé pieces online — 150
Become an online cord stockist — 151
BONUS — 153

Introduction

Macramé is a form of textile-making that uses knotting instead of weaving or knitting to create patterns and fabric. It dates back to the 13th century and was used as a way to decorate clothing and other textiles. In the late 1960s and early 1970s, macramé became popular again as a way to make wall hangings, plant hangers, and other home décor items.

Today, macramé is enjoying a resurgence in popularity as people are rediscovering the craft. It's a Fact that macramé can help in relaxation from today's stressful world and could be a good hobby or a skill to have. You will be able to create some really amazing crafts with your hands after reading this book.

We have first started by explaining the origin and history of macramé then to different tools and materials that may be required and also some of the basic and advanced knots and techniques that you need to know before you create something useful. And finally, some real-time projects that you can practice and trust me! They are very easy to follow.

The final chapter is about turning this new skill or hobby into a side hustle and we have discussed different ways to make money out of it.

Have a Good Read!!

Origins of Macramé

Origins of Macramé

Macramé is a form of textile-making that uses knotting instead of weaving or knitting to create patterns and fabric. It dates back to the 13th century and was used as a way to decorate clothing and other textiles. In the late 1960s and early 1970s, macramé became popular again as a way to make wall hangings, plant hangers, and other home décor items. Today, macramé is enjoying a resurgence in popularity as people are rediscovering the craft. In this chapter, we will explore the origins of macramé and how it has evolved over time.

Publications like "Sylvia's Book of Macramé Lace" offered instructions for the many ways macramé could be interpreted and use

WHAT IS MACRAMÉ

Macramé is a form of textile-making using knotting rather than weaving or knitting. The word macramé comes from the Arabic word migramah, meaning "embroidered cloth".

In macramé, patterns are created by knotting the cords in a variety of ways. Common knots used in macramé include the square knot, half hitch knot, and double half hitch knot. Macramé can be used to create a variety of items such as wall hangings, plant hangers, and even jewelry.

Photo Credits: (Anissa Ica)

Macramé was first used to decorate clothing and other textiles in Eastern cultures. It then spread to Europe, where it was used to adorn furniture and walls. In the 1970s, macramé became popular among bohemian and hippie fashion enthusiasts in North America and Europe as a way to make their own clothing and accessories.

Today, macramé is making a comeback as a trendy way to add texture and interest to home décor items such as wall hangings, plant hangers, and rugs.

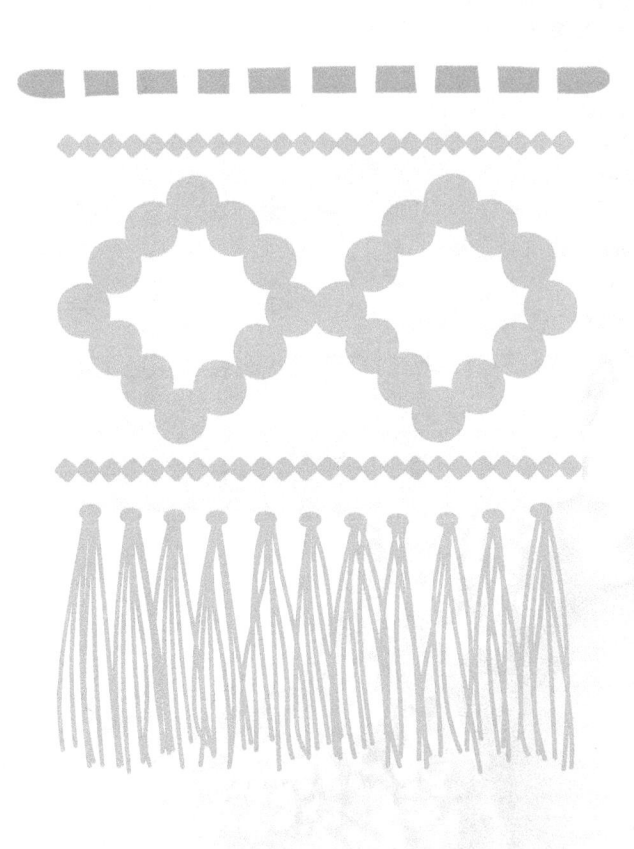

Wall Hanging

Plant Hanger

HISTORY OF MACRAMÉ

Macramé is believed to have originated in 13th-century Arabia, where it was used to decorate camel and horse saddles and other items. It then spread to Spain and Portugal, where it was used to adorn clothing and household items. By the 17th century, macramé had become popular in France and Italy.

In the mid-19th century, macramé was introduced to the United States by sailors who had learned the craft while traveling. During the Victorian era, it became fashionable for ladies to adorn their clothing and homes with macramé lace, which led to a boom in the popularity of the craft.

During the 1970s, macramé experienced a resurgence in popularity as a countercultural craft. It was used to make wall hangings, plant hangers, and other decorative items. Today, macramé is once again gaining in popularity as people are rediscovering its simple beauty.

HOW TO GET STARTED WITH MACRAMÉ

If you're interested in learning the art of macramé, there are a few things you'll need to get started. First, you'll need some supplies. You'll need a sturdy cord or rope, scissors, and something to use as a dowel or ring (this will be the center of your project). You can find all of these supplies at your local craft store.

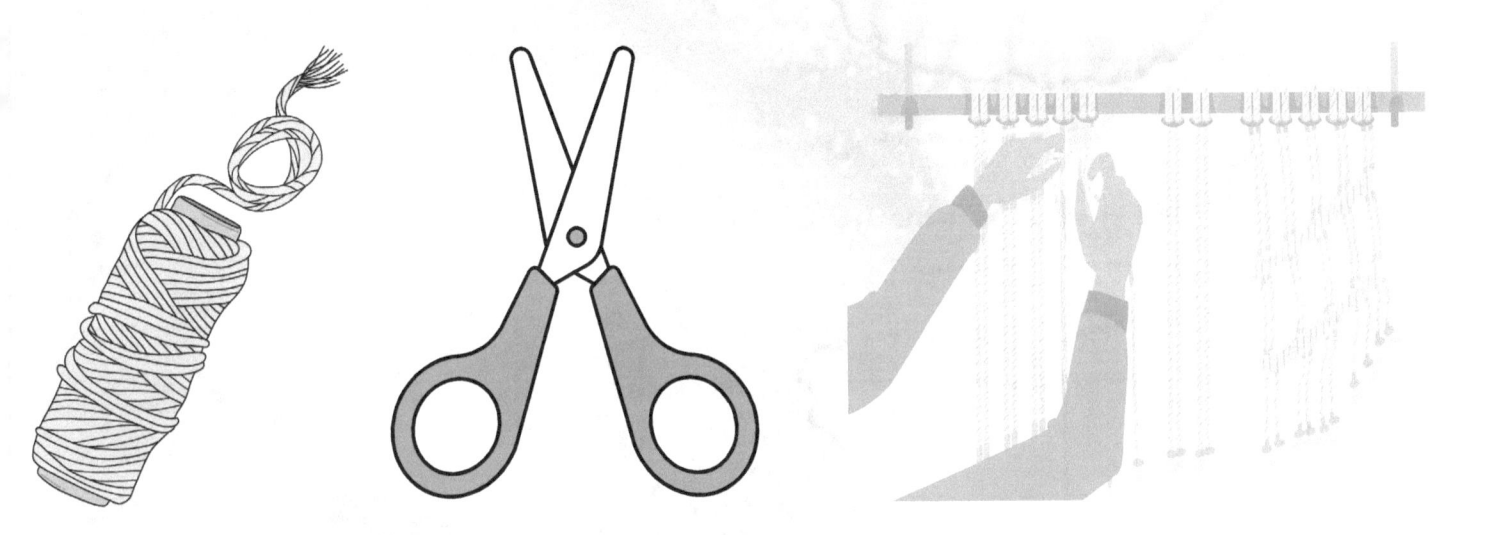

Once you have your supplies gathered, you're ready to start knotting! There are a variety of knots you can use in macramé, but the most common is the square knot. To tie a square knot, start by making a loop with one end of your cord. Cross the other end of the cord over the top of the loop, and then pull it through the loop (you should now have two loops). Take the top loop and put it over the bottom loop, then pull it through (you should now have one loop). Tighten both loops by pulling on them until they're snug against the cord. Repeat these steps to continue adding knots until your project is complete!

IS MACRAMÉ REALLY DIFFICULT TO LEARN?

Well, macramé may look a bit complicated and challenging but, it is really easy to learn and make some cool and interesting items even if you are a beginner. Like any other skill, it takes practice to become proficient at it. But with some patience and perseverance, anyone can learn how to make beautiful macramé projects.

We have designed this book in a way to make it as easy as possible to follow and starting from some easy projects to advanced ones, you will ace the art of making beautiful projects with macramé. With the completion of this book, you will not only learn the basics of macramé but have some beautiful decor items made with your hands that you can put for your personal use, sell them or gift them to your friends and family members.

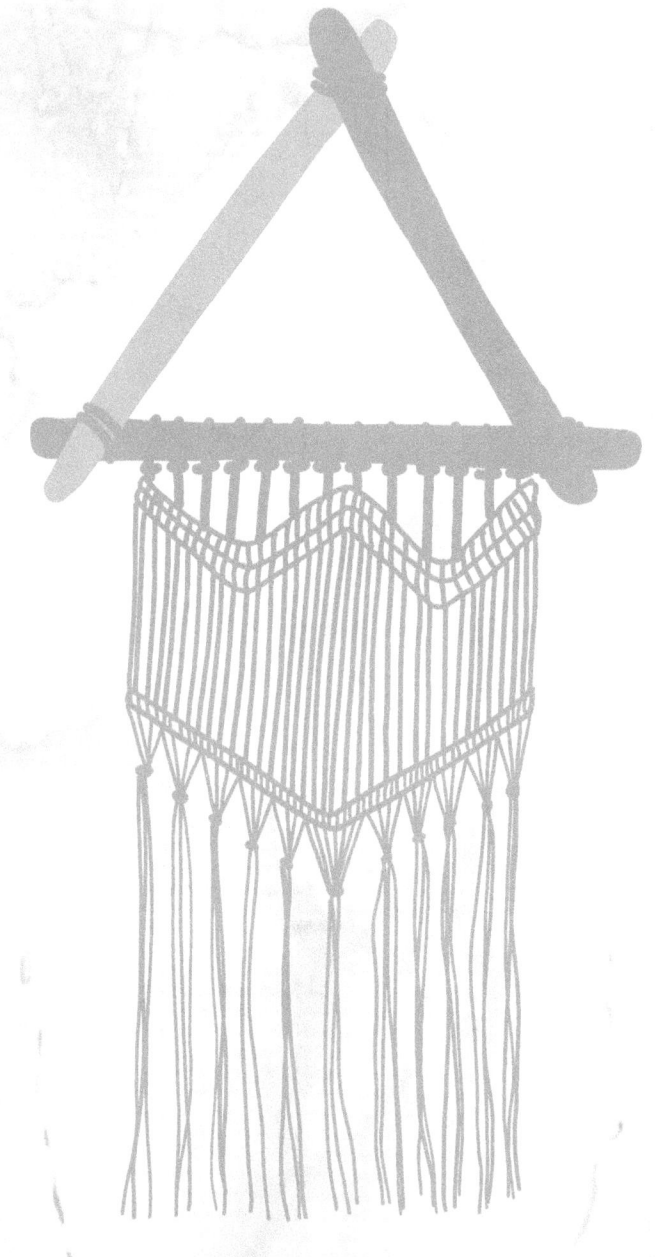

Tools and Materials

Tools and Materials

If you want to get into macramé, there are a few supplies you'll need to pick up. For starters, you'll need some sort of frame to tie your knots around. This can be anything from a dowel rod to a branch off a tree. You'll also need something to cut your rope with - a sharp pair of scissors will do the trick. And of course, you'll need rope! You can use any type of rope for macramé, but cotton or jute work well and are inexpensive. Once you have your supplies gathered, you're ready to start knotting!

I have put down a list of supplies and why you need them here in this chapter so make sure you read it carefully because without the knowledge I have put in this chapter, you won't be able to start your macramé journey.

YARN

There are a few different types of yarn that can be used for macramé projects. The most common type of yarn is cotton, which can be found in any craft store. wool and acrylic are also popular choices.

Cotton yarn is the best choice for beginners as it is easy to work with and knots will stay in place easily. It is also one of the most affordable options. Acrylic yarn is a synthetic option that is cheaper than wool and has a wide range of colors available. It can be difficult to work with though, so isn't always the best choice for beginners.

Wool yarn is the most expensive option but it is also the strongest and most durable. It can be tricky to work with as it can slip out of knots easily. However, it produces beautiful results so is worth considering if you're more experienced or are working on a larger project.

SCISSORS

When it comes to macramé, scissors are an essential tool. They are used to cut the cord, which is the main material used in this type of crafting. There are many different types of scissors that can be used for macramé, but the most important thing is to find a pair that is comfortable for you to use.

There are two main types of scissors that are commonly used for macramé: **fabric scissors and embroidery scissors**. Fabric scissors are larger and have blunt tips, which make them ideal for cutting thick materials like cord. Embroidery scissors are smaller and have sharp points, which make them better for precision cuts.

When choosing a pair of scissors, it is also important to consider the handle style. Some people prefer straight handles, while others prefer offset handles. Offset handles can be easier on your wrists and provide more control when cutting precise shapes.

No matter what type of scissors you choose, make sure to take care of them so they will last long enough to complete all your macramé projects!

MEASURING TOOLS

If you're just getting started with macramé, you'll need to gather a few supplies before you can start knotting. In addition to the cord or rope, you'll be using for your project, you'll need a way to measure it.

Here are a few different measuring tools that can be used for macramé:

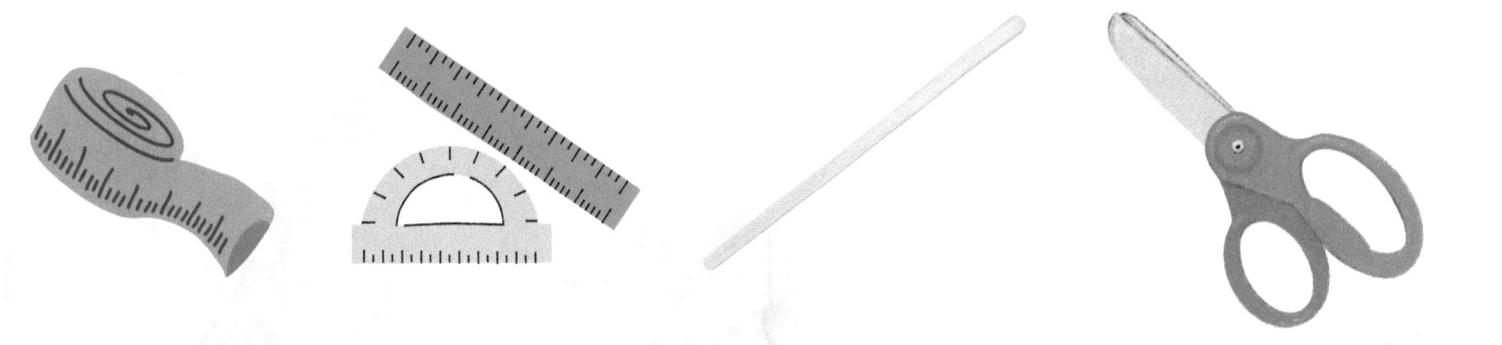

- **Measuring Tape**

This is the most common measuring tool and can be easily found at any hardware store.

- **Ruler:**

A ruler can also be used to measure macramé cord, though it's not as precise as a tape measure.

- **Yardstick:**

A yardstick can be helpful for measuring longer lengths of cord.

- **Scissors:**

You'll need a good pair of scissors to cut your cord to the desired length.

CORDS

There are many types of cords that can be used for macramé, and the best cord to use depends on the project you're working on.

For example, if you're making a wall hanging, you'll want to use a thicker cord so it will hold its shape well. But if you're making a plant hanger, you'll want to use a thinner cord so it's easy to tie knots in.

Here are some of the most popular types of cords used for macramé:

- **Jute:**

This is a natural fiber cord that's very strong and durable. It's perfect for projects that need to hold their shape well, like wall hangings.

- **Cotton:**

This is another natural fiber cord that's softer than jute. It's perfect for projects that require more delicate knotting, like plant hangers.

- **Polypropylene:**

This synthetic fiber cord is very strong and doesn't absorb water, making it perfect for outdoor projects.

- **Nylon:**

This synthetic fiber cord is also very strong, but it's much thinner than polypropylene so it's easier to work with.

- **Hemp:**

This natural fiber cord is similar to jute in terms of strength and durability. It's often used for larger projects like hammocks or rugs.

EMBROIDERY NEEDLES

Embroidery needles are the tools of the trade for macramé artists. They come in a variety of sizes and shapes, each designed for a specific purpose. The most common type of embroidery needle is the tapestry needle, which has a blunt tip and a large eye. This needle is perfect for weaving in and out of fabric without leaving behind any holes.

Other types of embroidery needles include beading needles, which have a small eye and sharp point; crewel needles, which are long and thin; and chenille needles, which are short and stout. No matter what type of needle you use, always thread it with a strong thread that won't break easily.

CLOTHES RAIL

One important macramé supply is a clothes rail. You can use any type of clothes rail, but we recommend one with an L-shape so that it's easy to hang your work while you're working on it. Clothes rails are also great for storing your finished pieces until you're ready to display them or give them away.

Let's Head to the

INTERESTING PART

Knots and Techniques

Knots and Techniques

The reason I was saying "let's head to the interesting part" was that in this chapter we are going to learn some of the most important knots and techniques after which the magic will happen and you will be making some amazing and creative crafts by your own, How Cool is that!

Before we start, you need to gather your supplies so that you are not distracted while you practice.

SUPPLIES AND MATERIALS

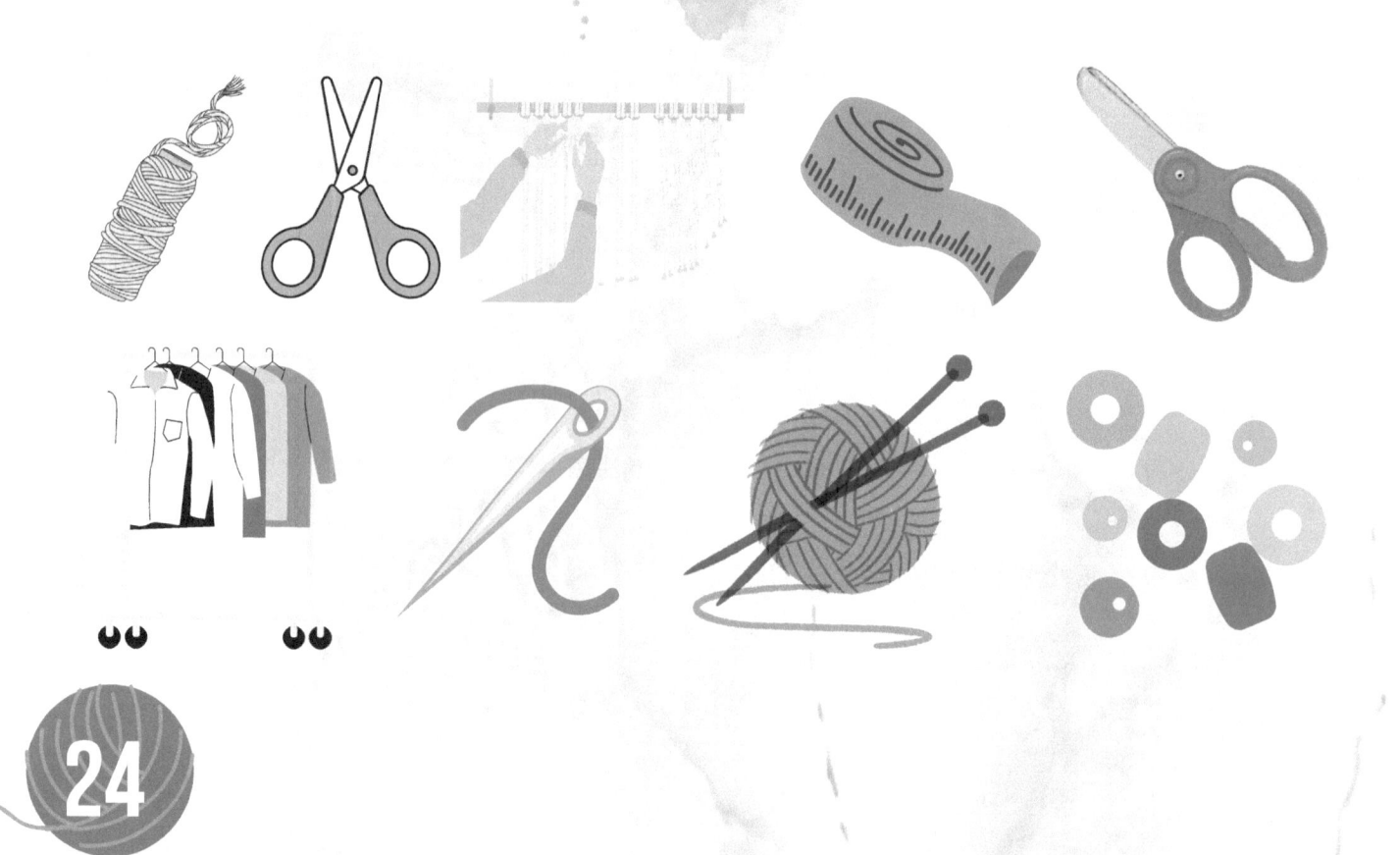

SQUARE KNOTS AND HALF KNOTS

There are two basic types of knots used in macramé: square knots and half knots. Square knots are the most common type of knot and are used to create a variety of different patterns. Half knots are less common but can be used to create more intricate designs.

SQUARE KNOTS

Square knots are the most basic type of knot, and are used to create a variety of different patterns. To tie a square knot, take two pieces of cord and cross them in the middle. Then, take the left piece of cord and put it over the right piece of cord. Next, take the right piece of cord and put it over the left piece of cord. Finally, pull both pieces of cord tight.

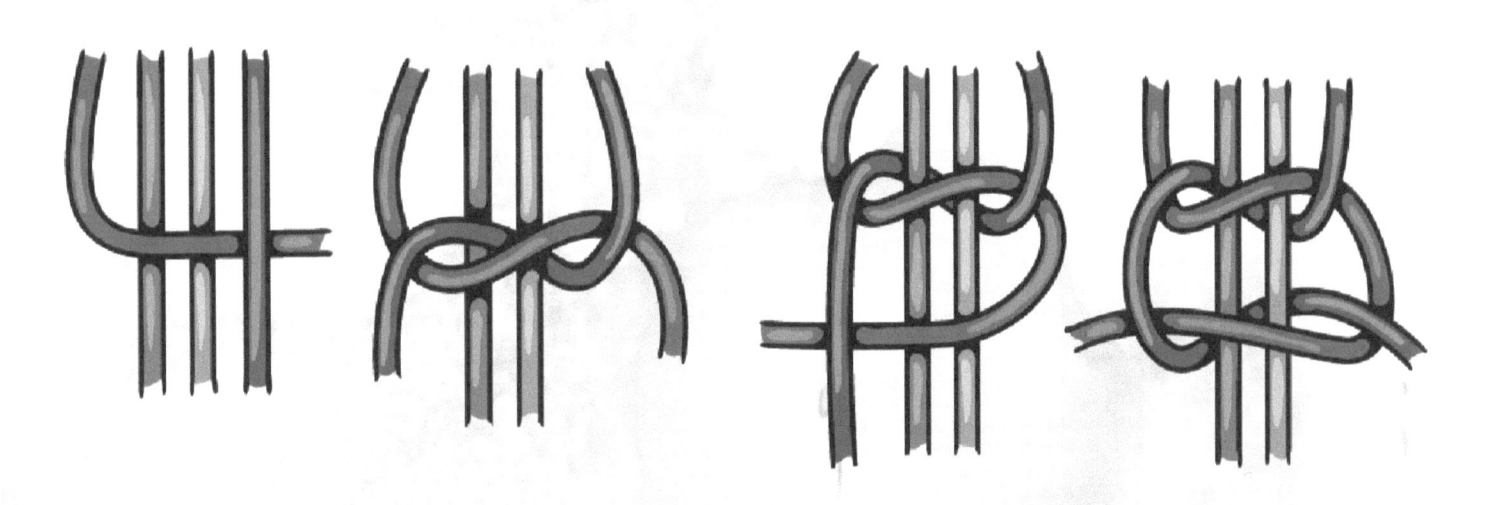

HALF KNOTS

Half knots are less common than square knots, but can be used to create more intricate designs. To tie a half knot, take two pieces of cord and cross them in the middle. Then, take the left piece of cord and put it under the right piece of cord. Next, take the right piece of cord and put it over the left piece of cord. Finally, pull both pieces of cord tight.

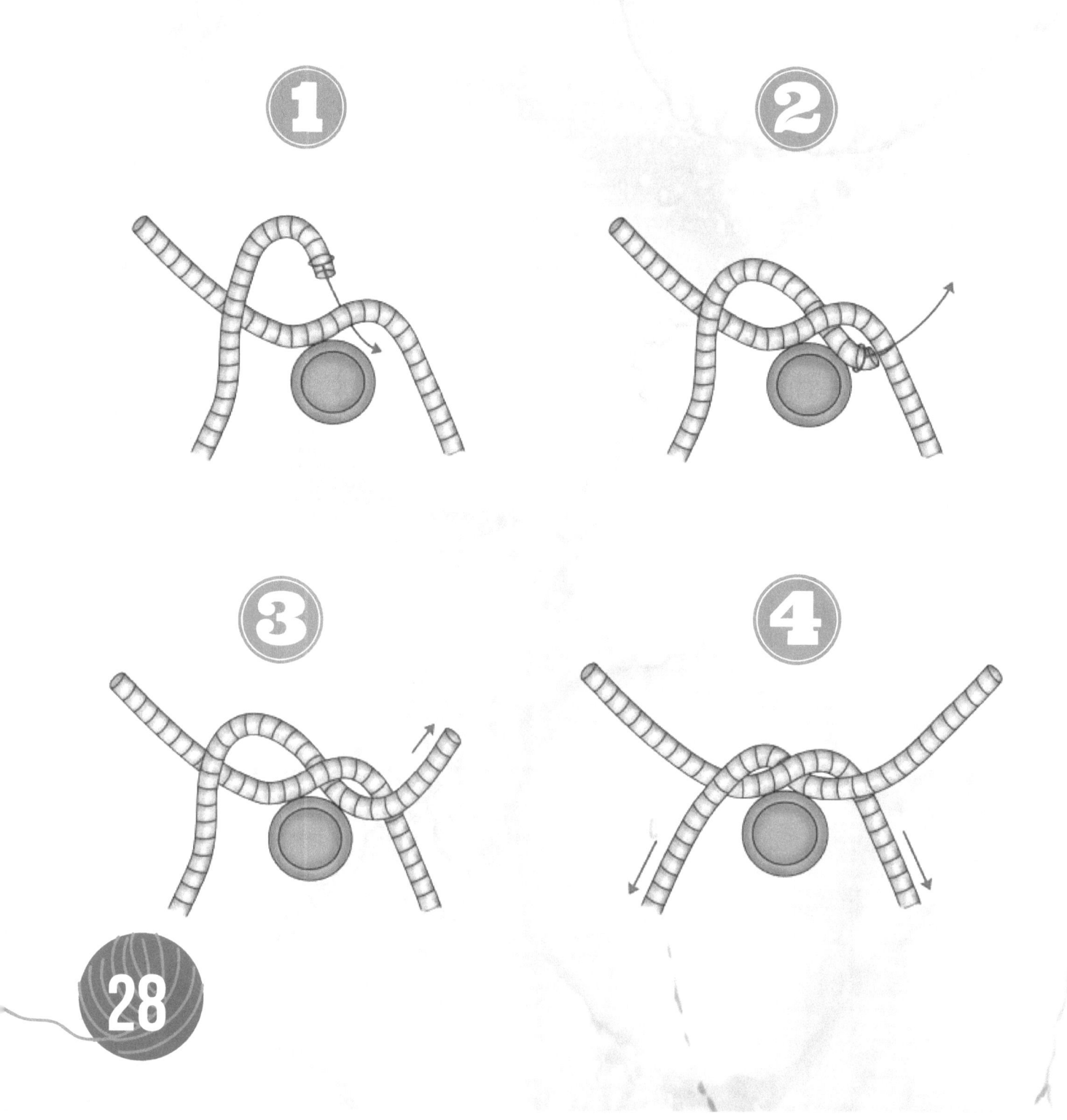

SPIRAL STICH

The spiral stitch is one of the most popular stitches used in macramé. It is created by looping the cord around itself in a spiral pattern. This stitch can be used to create a variety of different designs, including bracelets, rings, and even wall hangings.

To create a spiral stitch, start by creating a loop with your cord. Then, take the end of the cord and wrap it around the loop several times. Continue wrapping the cord around itself until you have reached the desired length. To secure the spiral stitch, simply tie off the end of the cord.

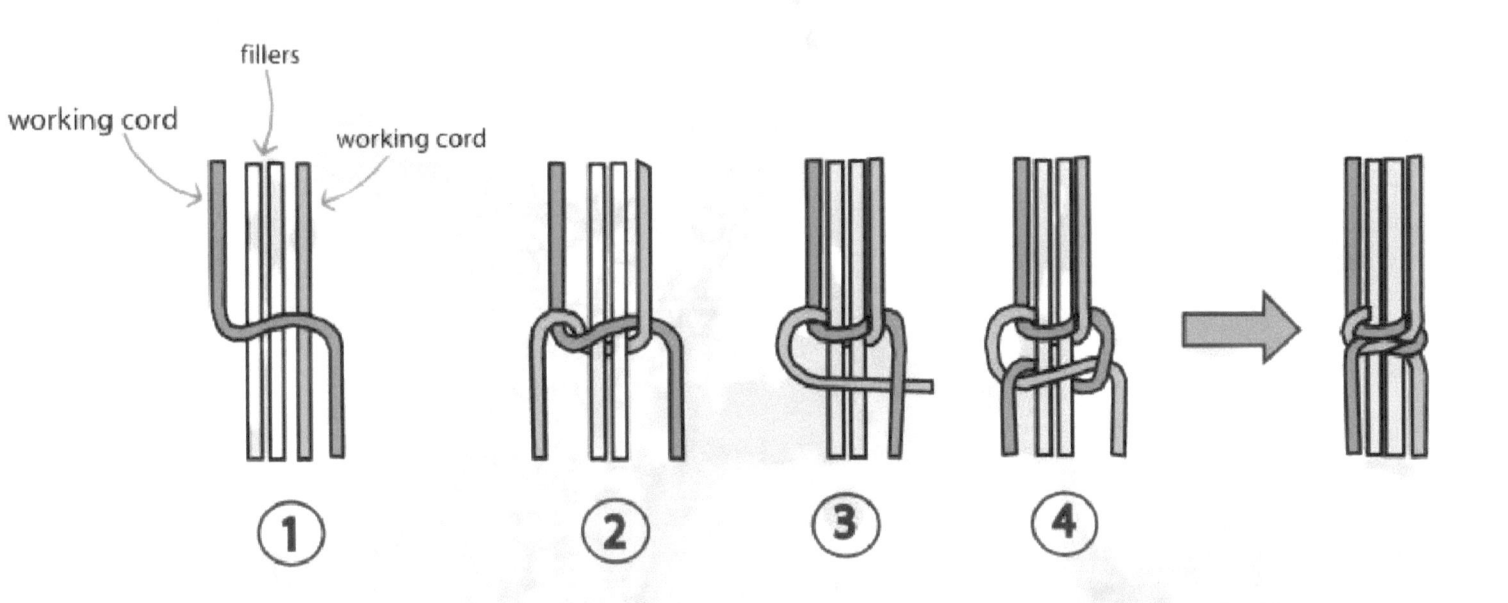

① ② ③ ④

CLOVE HITCH

The clove hitch is one of the most basic and versatile knots used in macramé. It is created by wrapping the cord around an object (such as a dowel or pole) and then tying the ends together. The clove hitch can be used to create a variety of patterns and shapes, and is often used as a starting point for more complex designs.

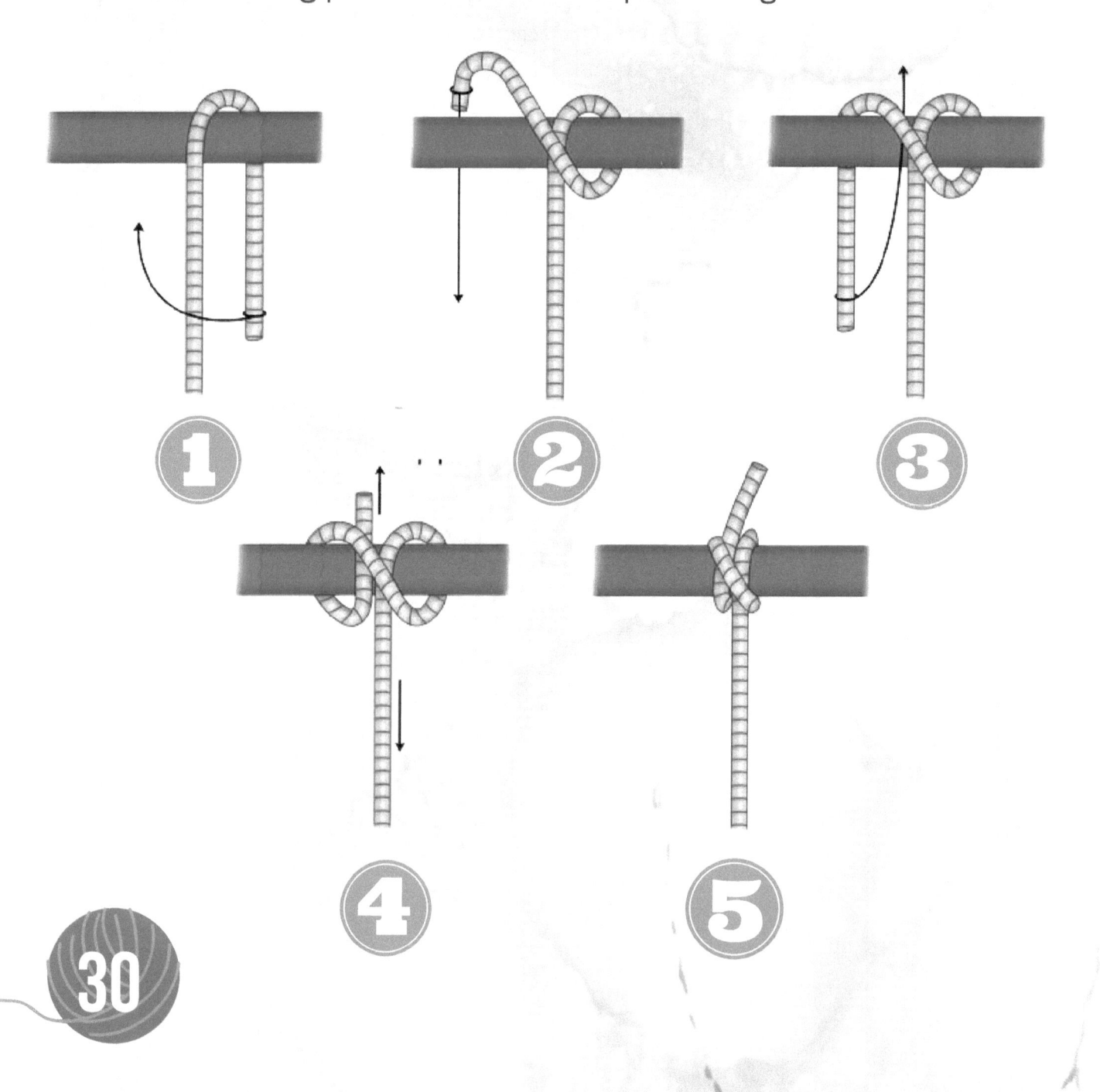

① ② ③ ④ ⑤

OVERHAND KNOT

The overhand knot is one of the most basic knots used in macramé. This knot is often used to create a starting point for other macramé knots and patterns. It can also be used on its own to create simple decorations.

To make this knot, start with a long piece of rope or cord. Make a loop in the center of the rope, then pass the working end over the standing end of the rope. Pull the working end through the loop that is formed, then pull it tight. You can adjust the size of the loop by pulling on either end of the rope.

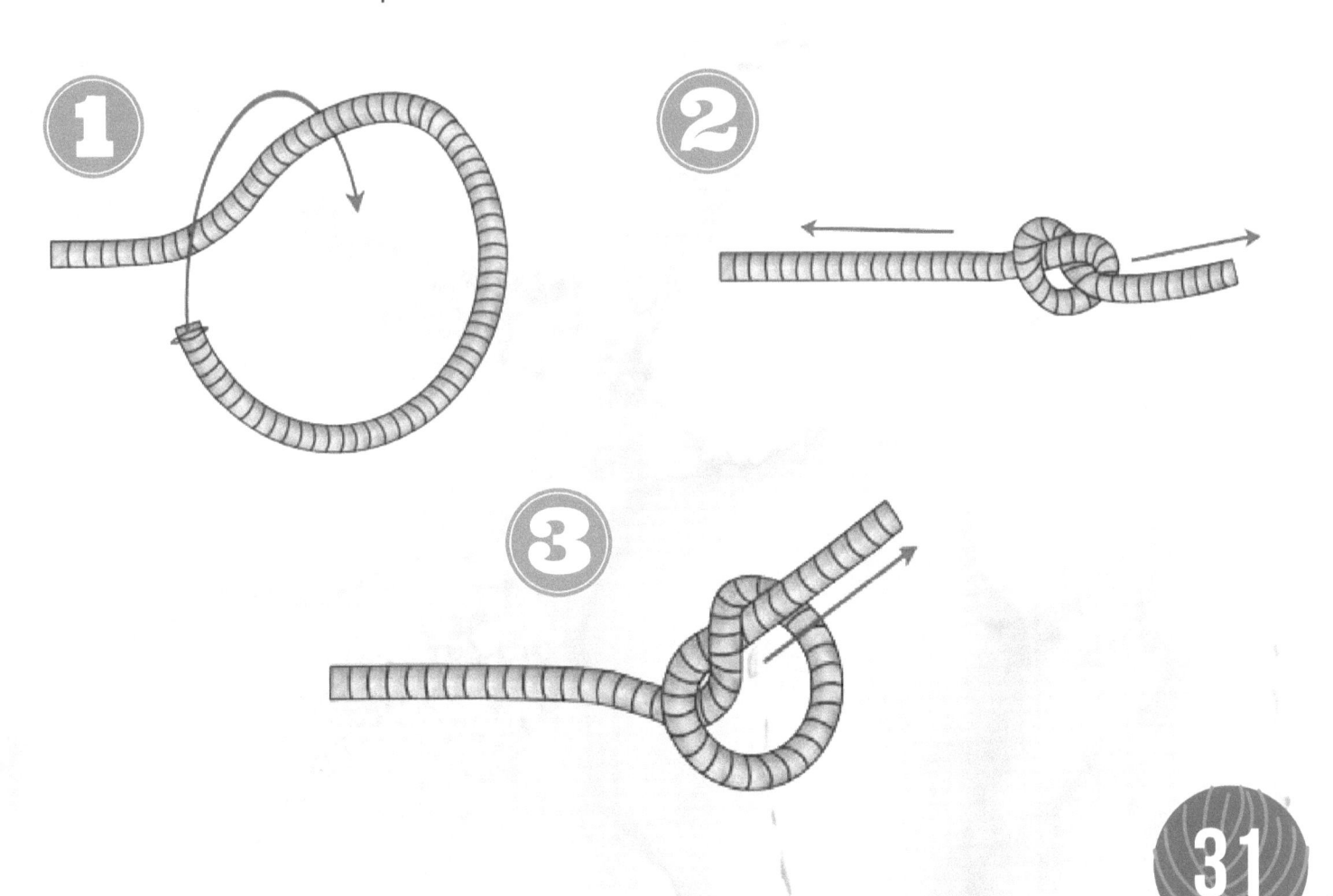

GATHERING KNOT

The gathering knot is one of the most commonly used knots in macramé, and it's a great knot to use for beginners.

The gathering knot is created by tying a simple knot around two cords. To create the knot, start by holding the two cords together and making a loop. Then, take the top cord and make a second loop around the bottom cord. Finally, pull both loops tight.

The gathering knot can be used to create a variety of patterns, including diamond shapes, stars, and hearts. It's also a great knot to use for framing other macramé knots or patterns.

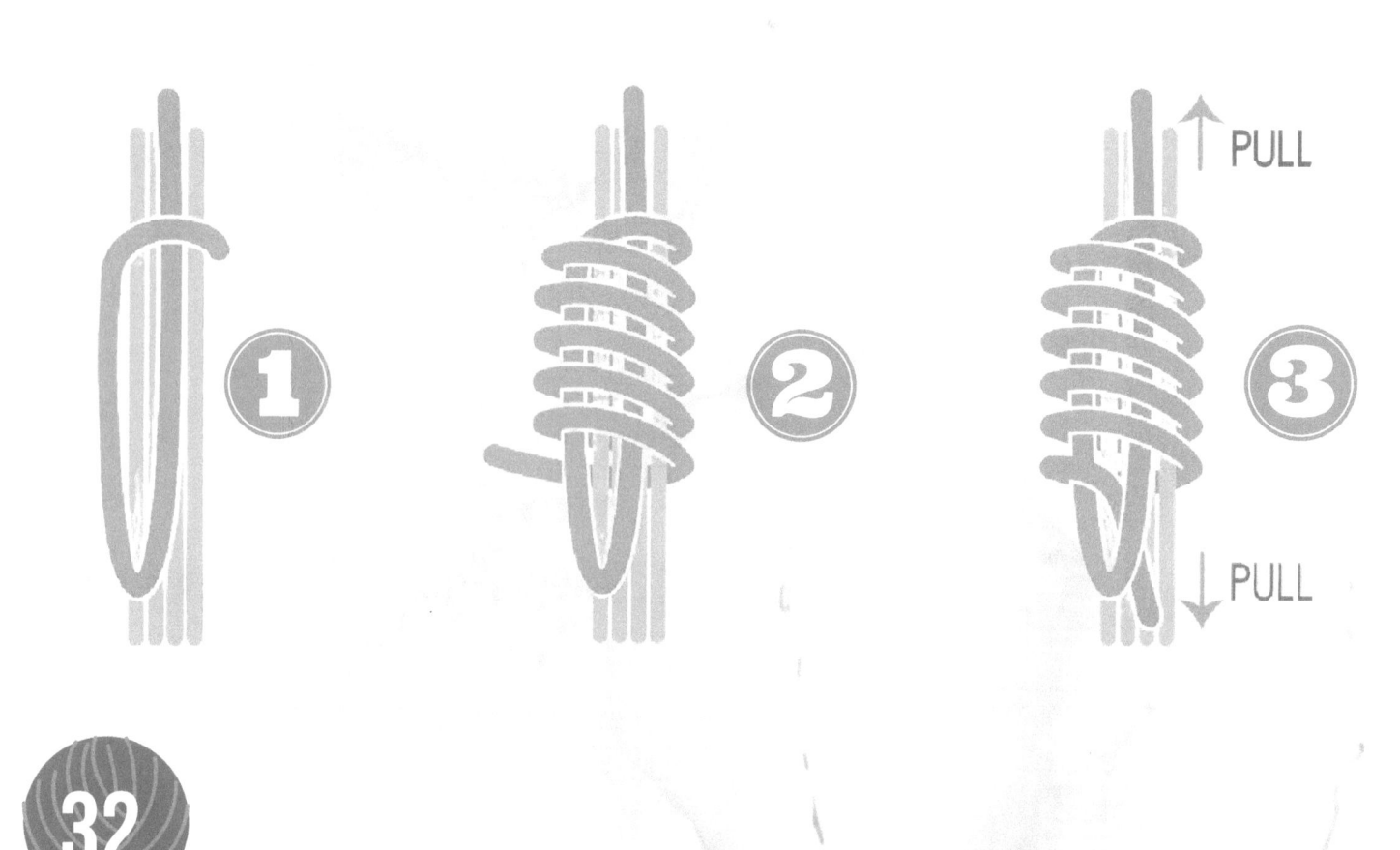

WRAPPING KNOT

There are many different knots that can be used in macramé, but the wrapping knot is one of the most versatile. This knot can be used to create a variety of shapes and patterns, and is also great for joining two pieces of cord together.

To make a wrapping knot, start by tying a basic knot in the center of your cord. Then, take one end of the cord and wrap it around the other end, making sure to cross over the center knot. Continue wrapping the cord around itself until you reach the desired length. Finally, tie another knot at the end to secure it in place.

Wrapping knots are simple to make but can be very strong, so they're perfect for use in bracelets, keychains, or other projects where you need a little extra durability. And because they're so easy to customize, you can really let your creativity shine through when using this type of knot!

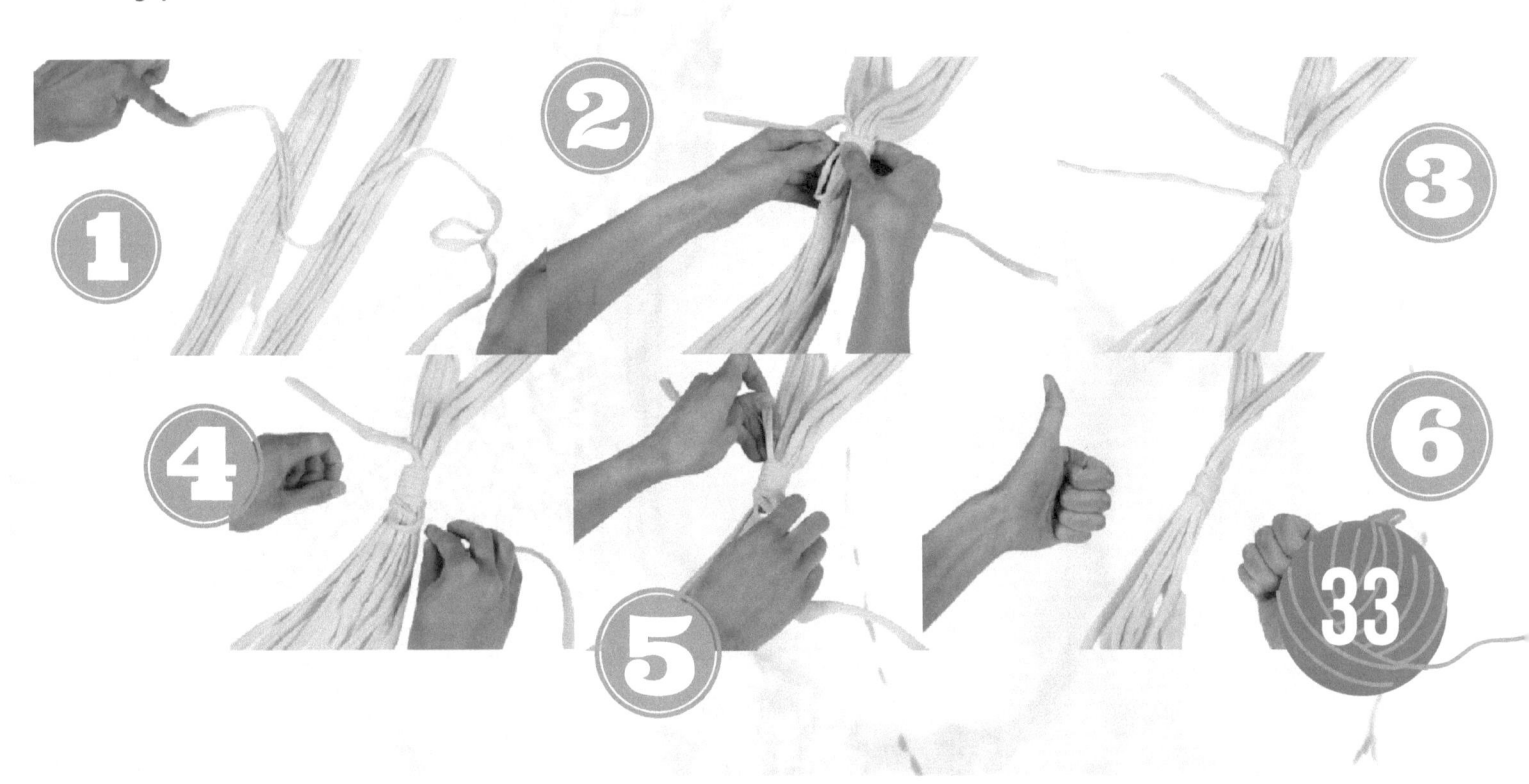

HALF HITCH

A half hitch is a basic macramé knot that is often used to create patterns and texture in a design. It is created by passing the working cord over the base cord, then under the base cord, and finally over the top of the working cord. This creates a loop around the base cord, which can be tightened or loosened to create different effects.

Half hitches are often used in conjunction with other knots, such as square or spiral knots, to create more complex patterns. They can also be used alone to create simple designs. Half hitches can be worked in rows or columns, and can be spaced closely together or farther apart to create different effects.

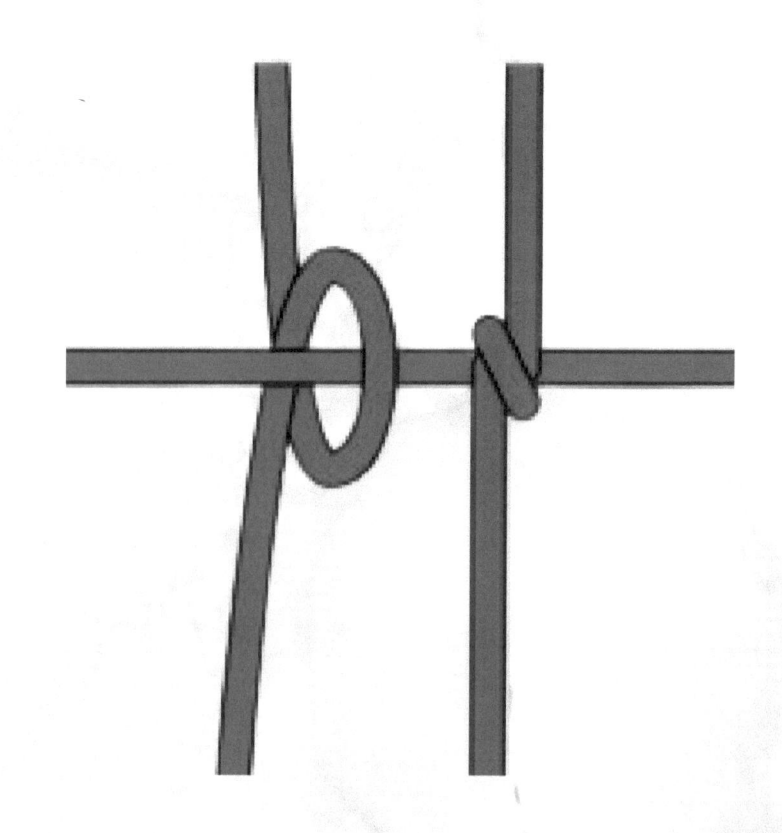

COW HITCH KNOT

The Cow Hitch knot is one of the most commonly used knots in macramé. It's a simple, yet versatile knot that can be used to create a variety of different patterns and designs.

To tie a Cow Hitch knot, start by tying a basic knot in the center of your rope or cord. Then, take the left side of the rope and make a loop around the right side of the rope. Next, take the right side of the rope and make a loop around the left side of the rope. Finally, pull both loops tight.

The Cow Hitch knot can be used to create a wide variety of patterns and designs in macramé. To get started, try using this knot to create a basic square or diamond shape. Once you're comfortable with the Cow Hitch knot, you can experiment with different sizes and shapes to create more complex designs.

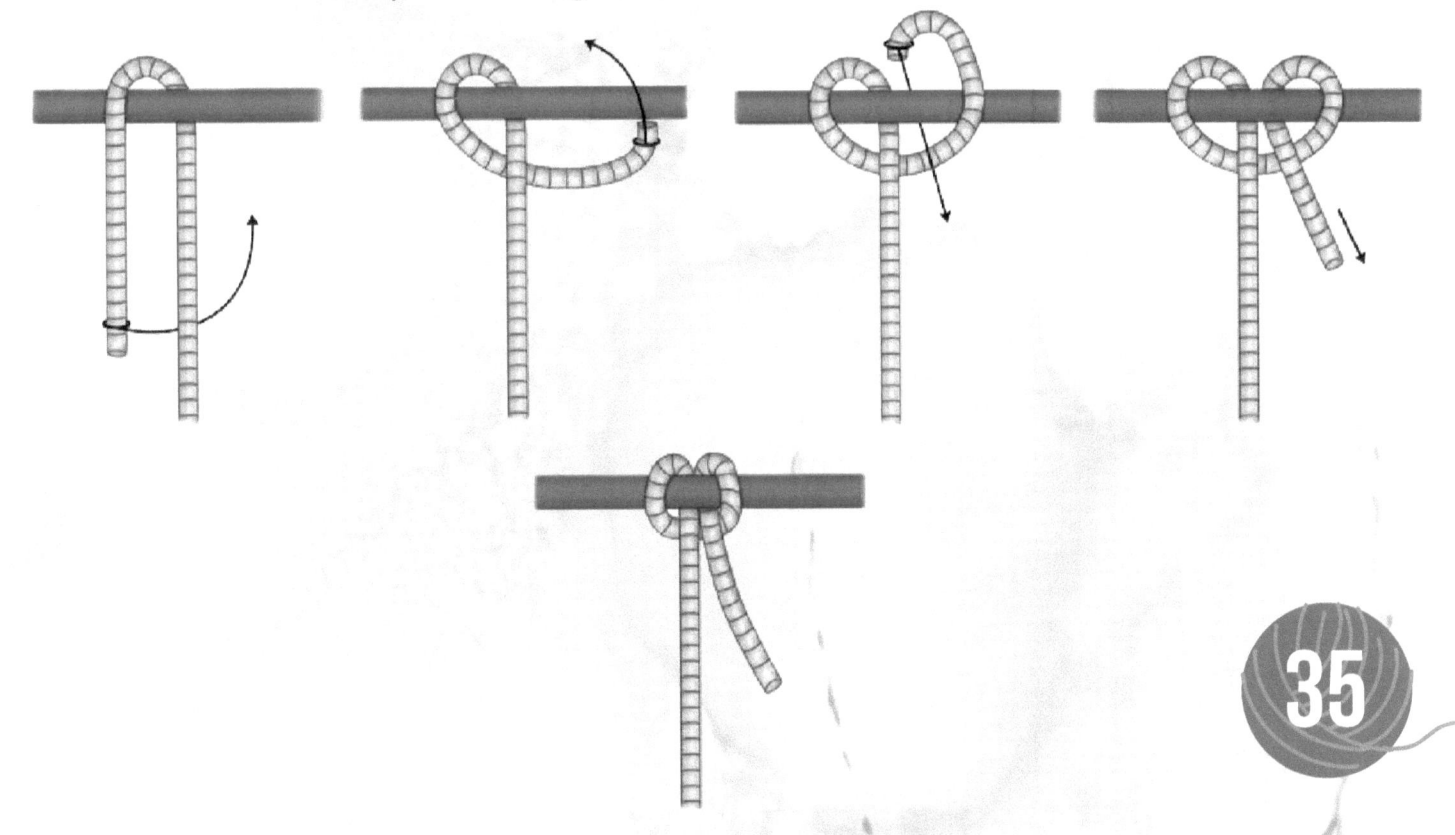

35

BARREL KNOT

The barrel knot is one of the most popular knots used in macramé. It is a very versatile knot that can be used to create a variety of different patterns and designs. The barrel knot is created by tying a loop in the center of a cord or rope. The loop can be created with either a loop knot or a lark's head knot.

Once the loop is created, the ends of the cord or rope are passed through the loop from the top. Then, each end is passed over the other end and pulled through the loop. The ends are then pulled tight to secure the knot.

The barrel knot is often used to create fringes on macramé projects. It can also be used to create tassels, pendants, and other decorative elements.

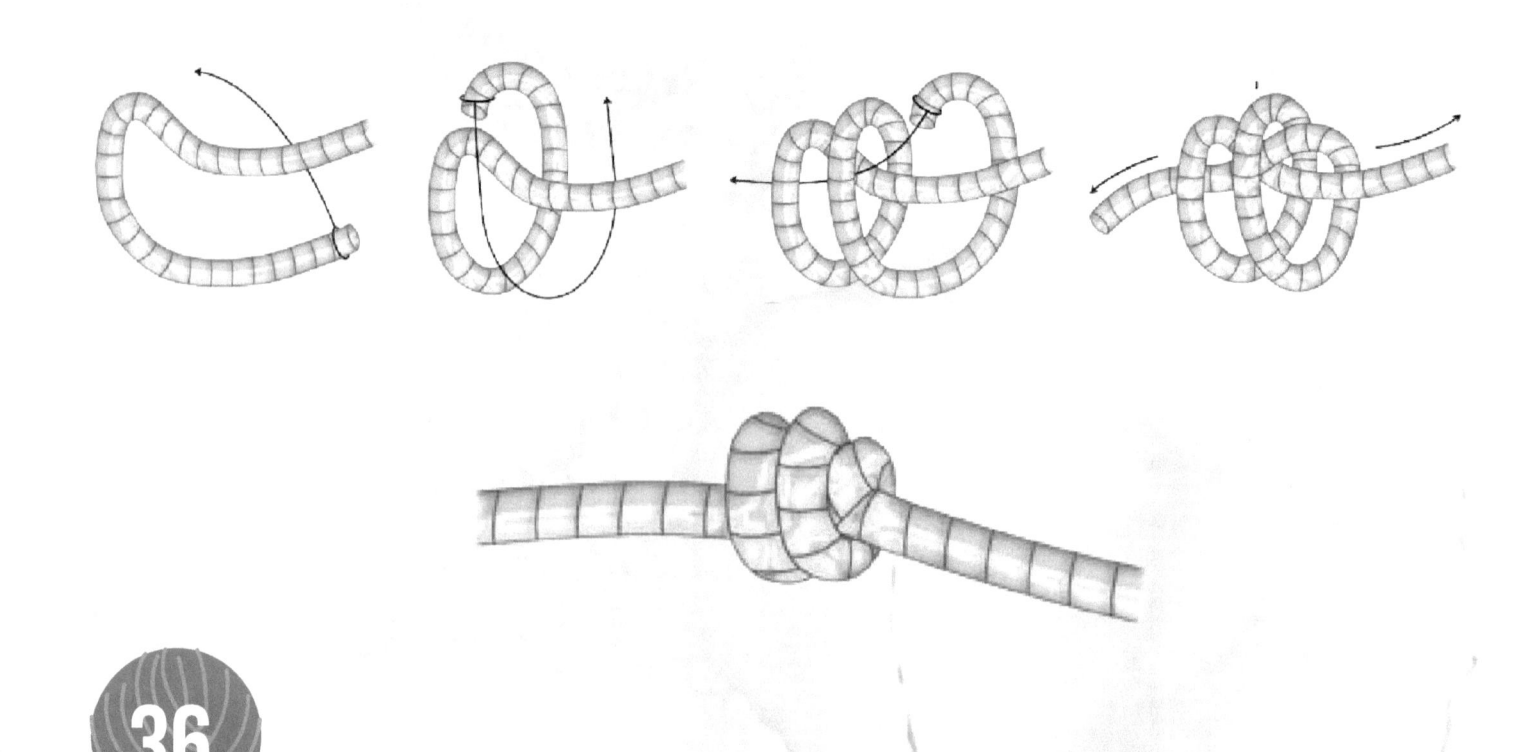

CONSTRICTOR KNOT

The Constrictor Knot is one of the most versatile knots in macramé, and can be used in a variety of ways. It's simple to tie, and can be easily adjusted to create different effects.

The Constrictor Knot is commonly used to secure cord ends, or to create a "fringe" effect on a piece of macramé. To tie a Constrictor Knot, start by tying a basic knot (such as a Square Knot) in the cord. Then, take the left side of the cord and wrap it around the right side, twice. Finally, pull the left side of the cord through the loop created by the wraps (as shown in the photo below).

The number of wraps around the cord can be varied to create different effects. For example, you could try wrapping the cord around three times instead of two. Or, you could experiment with using different types of knots (such as Half Hitch knots) in conjunction with the Constrictor Knot.

There are endless possibilities for using the Constrictor Knot in macramé – so get creative and see what you can come up with!

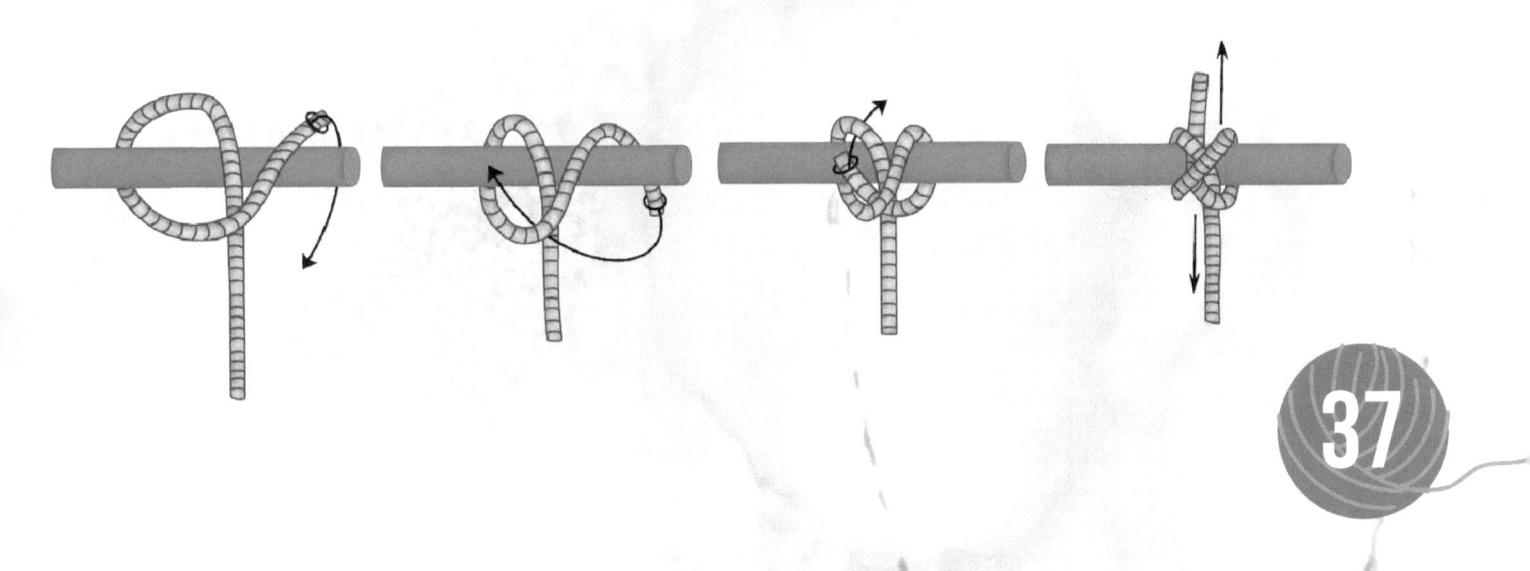

JOSEPHINE KNOT

The Josephine Knot is one of the most popular knots used in macramé. It's named after its inventor, Josephine knot creator Carol Bradley. The Josephine knot is created by tying two loops together in an overhand knot, then passing the end of one loop through the other loop and pulling tight. This forms a secure, strong knot that can be used to join two pieces of cord or rope together.

The Josephine knot is a versatile knot that can be used in a variety of ways in macramé projects. It's often used to create decorative elements like fringes and tassels, or to join two pieces of fabric together.

CHINESE CROWN KNOT

The Chinese Crown Knot is a beautiful and intricate macramé knot that can be used to create stunning decorative pieces. This knot is created by tying two cords together in a special way, resulting in a complex and eye-catching pattern.

This knot is relatively easy to learn, and once you know how to tie it, you can use it to create all sorts of different macramé projects. It's perfect for creating jewelry, wall hangings, plant hangers, and more.

If you're interested in learning how to tie the Chinese Crown Knot, there are plenty of online tutorials and resources that can help you out. Once you've mastered this knot, you'll be able to add a touch of elegance to any macramé project you undertake!

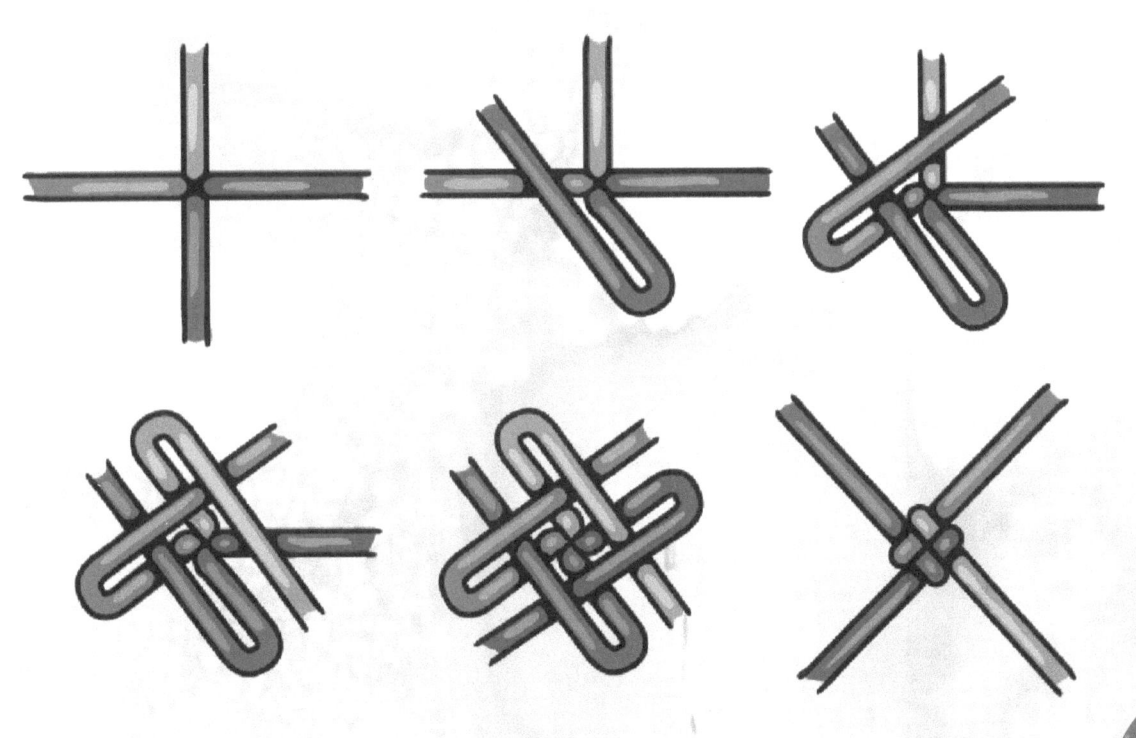

Things to Avoid in Macramé

Things to Avoid in Macramé

Macramé is a beautiful, intricate craft that can be used to create stunning home decor, accessories, and more. But like any craft, there are certain things you should avoid if you want your project to turn out right. In this chapter, we will explore some of the things you should avoid when working with macramé. From using the wrong type of cord to not planning your design ahead of time, read on to learn more about what can go wrong with your macramé project and how to avoid it.

When you're first starting out with macramé, it's easy to make some common mistakes. To help you avoid them, we've put together a list of the five most common mistakes beginners make, and how to avoid them.

1) CUTTING CORD TOO SHORT

If you're new to macramé, it's easy to make the mistake of cutting your cord too short. This can be frustrating because it means you have to start over with a new piece of cord. To avoid this mistake, be sure to measure your cord before you cut it. It's also a good idea to leave a little extra length so that you can adjust if necessary.

2) NOT BUYING ENOUGH CORD

One of the most common mistakes people make when starting out with macramé is not buying enough cord. It may seem like a small thing, but running out of cord in the middle of a project can be really frustrating. Make sure to buy at least 10% more cord than you think you need, just to be safe.

3) FORGETTING TO PRACTICE KNOTS

Forgetting to practice knots may seem like a small thing, but it can make a big difference in the overall look of your finished project.

If you're not sure how to tie a particular knot, take some time to practice it before you start your project. That way, you'll be able to get the hang of it and avoid any potential mistakes.

4) PULLING YOUR KNOTS TOO TIGHT OR NOT TIGHT ENOUGH

When it comes to macramé, one of the most common mistakes is either pulling your knots too tight or not tight enough. If you pull your knots too tight, it can cause your fabric to pucker and warp, making it difficult to work with. On the other hand, if you don't pull your knots tight enough, they can become loose and slip out of place.

To avoid this mistake, it's important to find a happy medium when pulling your knots. You should make sure they're tight enough so that they won't come undone, but not so tight that they distort the fabric. With a little practice, you'll be able to get the perfect tension on your knots every time!

5) GIVING UP

One of the most common mistakes people make when learning macramé is giving up too soon. It can be easy to get frustrated when your knots don't look perfect or your project isn't turning out the way you envisioned it. But with a little bit of practice and patience, you'll be able to create beautiful pieces of macramé art. So, don't give up – keep practicing and you'll eventually get the hang of it!

NEVER give up!

SOME COMMON MACRAMÉ ERRORS AND THEIR TROUBLESHOOTING

Some of the most common macramé errors include incorrect knotting, fraying cord, and uneven tension. Here are some tips on how to troubleshoot these problems:

INCORRECT KNOTTING

One of the most common macramé errors is incorrect knotting. This can cause your project to loosen over time or even come undone completely. To avoid this, be sure to tighten each knot as you go and double check your work before moving on to the next step.

FRAYING CORD

Another common error is the fraying cord. This can happen if you use a lower-quality cord or if you don't seal the ends of your cord before beginning your project. To avoid fraying, be sure to use a high quality cord and seal the ends with heat shrink tubing or a similar product.

UNEVEN TENSION

If your cords are not all the same tension, it can cause your project to look uneven. To fix this, simply adjust the tension on each cord until they are all even.

Macramé Projects

Macramé Projects

Now comes the most interesting part of this book, we will make some beautiful decorative items for our home, plants, holidays and for other items in our houses. Now that you know everything about the basics from its history to different tools, materials, knots and techniques, we will be using the same knowledge and will apply to our amazing projects in this chapter. You can skip to any project you think is easier and best to start with.

Just keep in mind, you may not make it that perfect at the first attempt. Practice it as much as you can because perfection comes from practice and in fact if you just try to do it perfect for the first time, you may fail badly and loose confidence. So we always recommend to just make a lot of imperfect items than one perfect, you will learn alot more than mentioned in this book! And why am I saying that? Its my personal experience and all macramé artists you might be following, they have all gone through failures and practice makes them aside from others.

To make it easier for you to navigate through the projects we are going to make in this book, I have divided them into different categories like DIY Macramé Projects for Home, Planters, Holidays and some Accessories. Saying it again, you can start with any project that seems easier to you. Let's get started!

For Home

WALL HANGING

Materials Required

- 188 Yards of 4mm 3 Strand Cotton Macramé Cord
- Stick, driftwood or dowel measuring 20 Inches

Tools

- Measuring Tape
- Scissors

Photo Credits: (joyfulderivatives)

Instructions

Step 1 - Cut the Cord

First, you will have to measure and cut all of your cord for the project. Now, cut 28 strands and each measuring 20 feet and one strand of 3 feet.

Photo Credits: (joyfulderivatives)

Step 2 - Attach Cord to Stick

Now, you will have to attach all of the cord strings to the stick and starting from the 3 feet string which will be used to hang up your work.

To start, tie a knot onto one end of the stick, about an inch or so away from the end.

In order to tighten and secure the cord, pull up on the long end of the cord and tighten the smaller end by pushing the top loop down and pulling the small end tight.

You will end up creating a nice, tight lark's head knot! Now, do the same thing on the other side with the other end of the cord.

Photo Credits: (joyfulderivatives)

Next, hang up the stick you just prepared on the wall using a nail or a hook and attach 28 long cords evenly across the dowel using the lark's head knot.

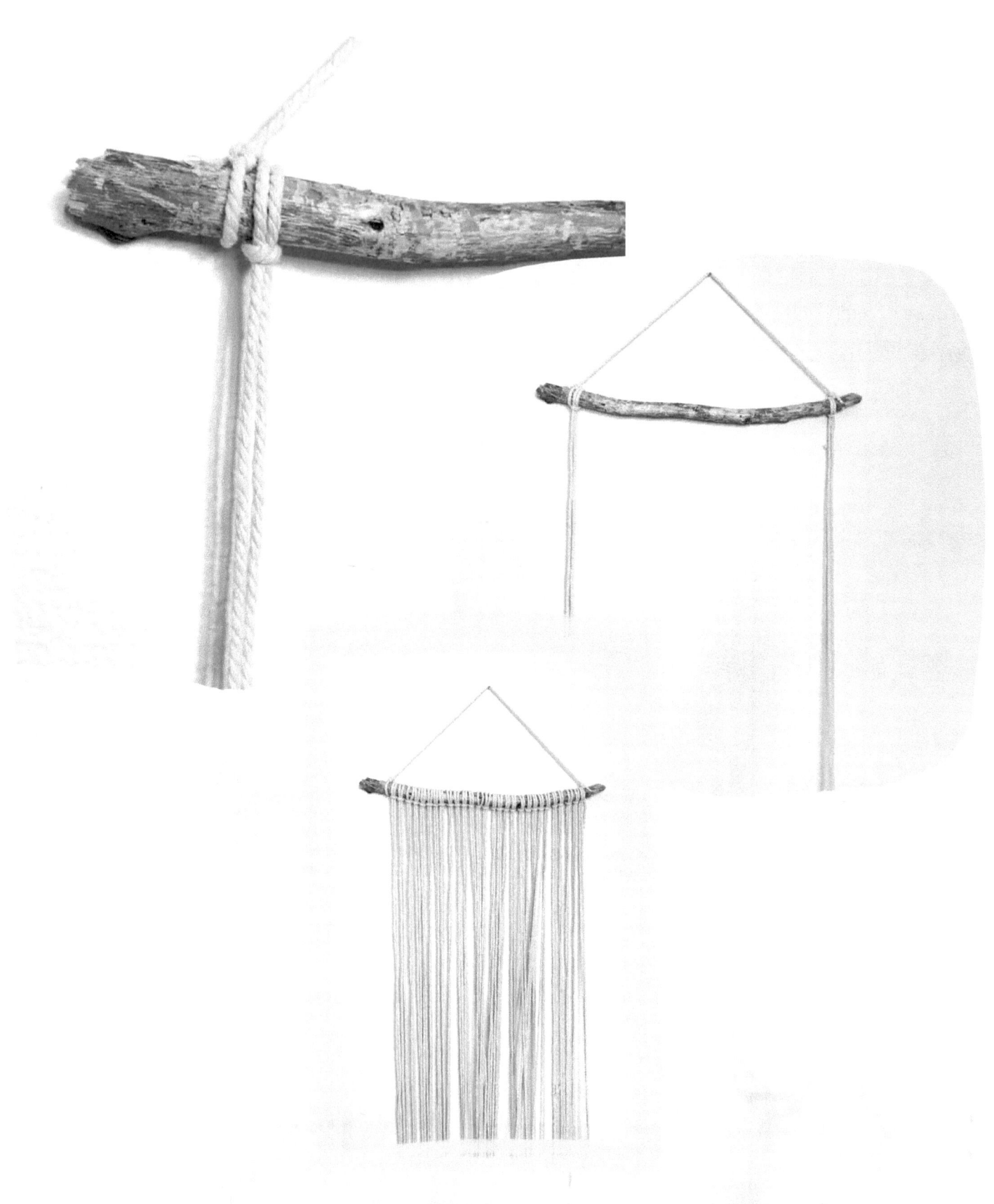

Photo Credits: (joyfulderivatives)

Step 3 - Create Triangle Using Square Knots and DHH

First, Create a square knot using two of the attached cords, four total strands, and continue making square knots until you get to the end. I usually go from left to right but you can go from any side.

Photo Credits: (joyfulderivatives)

Skip the first two strands of the first cord. Split the four strands from the first square knot in half and take the first two strands of the second knot.

You should now have two strands from each of the square knots, 4 strands in total.

Now, make a square knot below and in between the above square knots.

Do this all the way to the end, leaving the last two stands of cord unused.

Photo Credits: (joyfulderivatives)

Continue decreasing two strands on either end until you have one final knot at the bottom, making a triangle.

Photo Credits: (joyfulderivatives)

Double Half Hitch Knot (DHH)

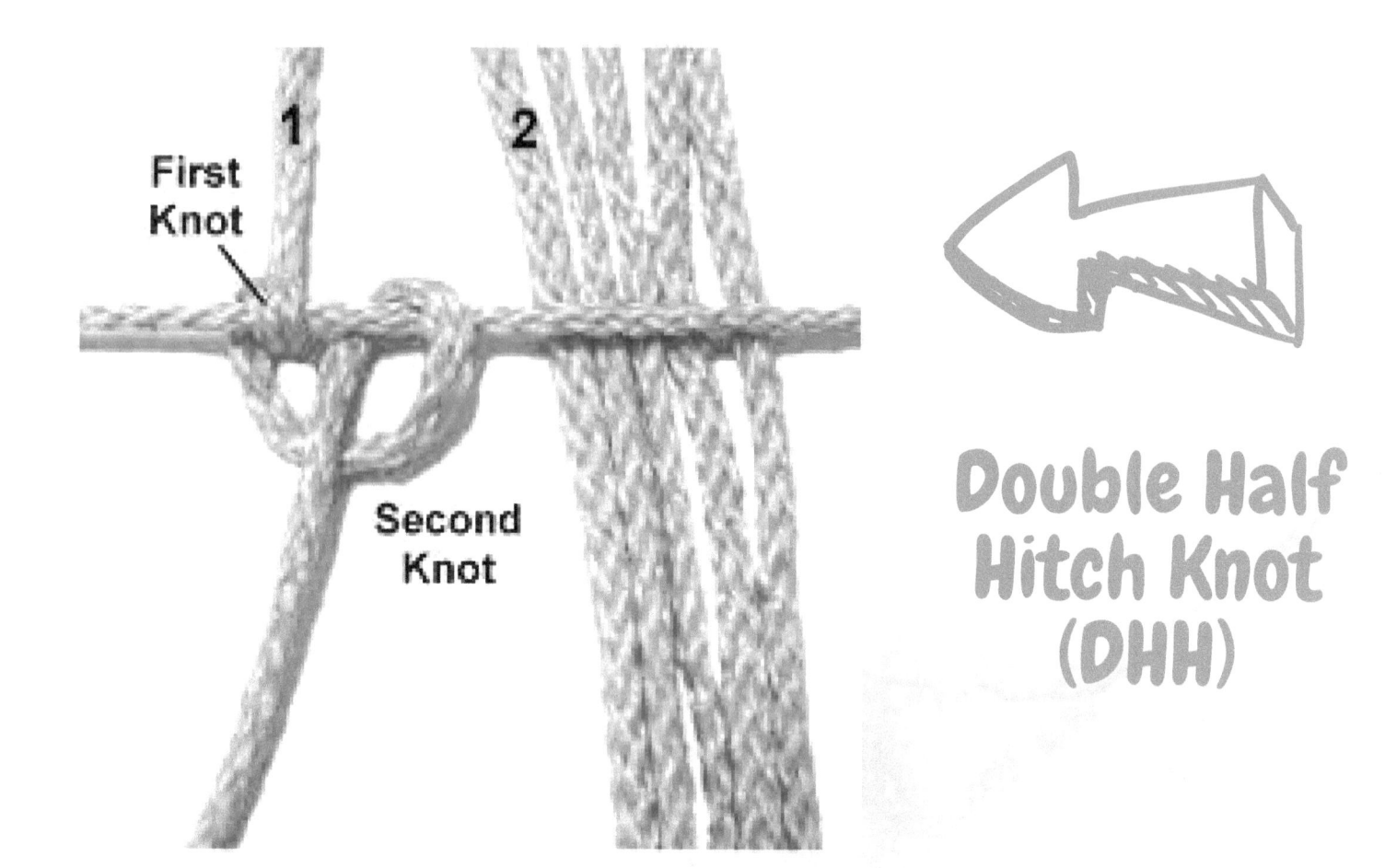

First Knot 1
Second Knot 2

Now, we will do DHH along the line of the triangle to create a nice definition to the triangle

Photo Credits: (joyfulderivatives)

The far left cord will be your holding cord. DHH until you reach the middle of the triangle. Your last DHH on the left side should use half of the last knot in the triangle; the other half will be used on the right side.

Photo Credits: (joyfulderivatives)

Now, DHH down the right side using the far right cord as your holding cord. Once you have got to the bottom and have used all of your remaining working cords, used the right holding cord as your holding cord and the left holding cord as your working cord. Create the last DHH and finish the triangle.

Step 4 - Spiral Knots

Create a line of spiral knots going down each side of the triangle. Each spiral knot will have 10 total knots. On the left side, have them be right spiraling knots by only doing the first part of a square knot, using the "4" method.

Photo Credits: (joyfulderivatives)

For the right side spiral knots, you'll want them spiraling toward the left. Do this by only using the backwards "4" knot, like you do on the second part of a square knot. This will make the spiral go in the other direction.

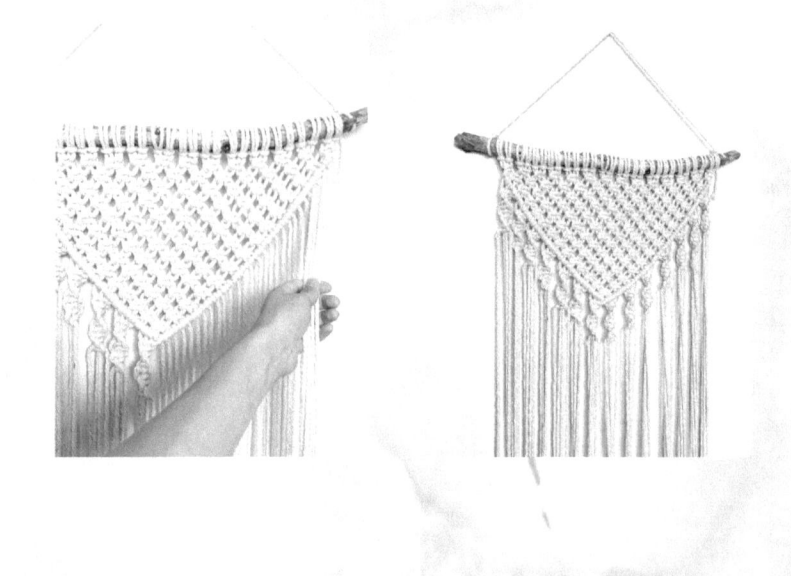

Now we will close off this part of the triangle using the DHH. Join the two ends together as you did the top part of the triangle.

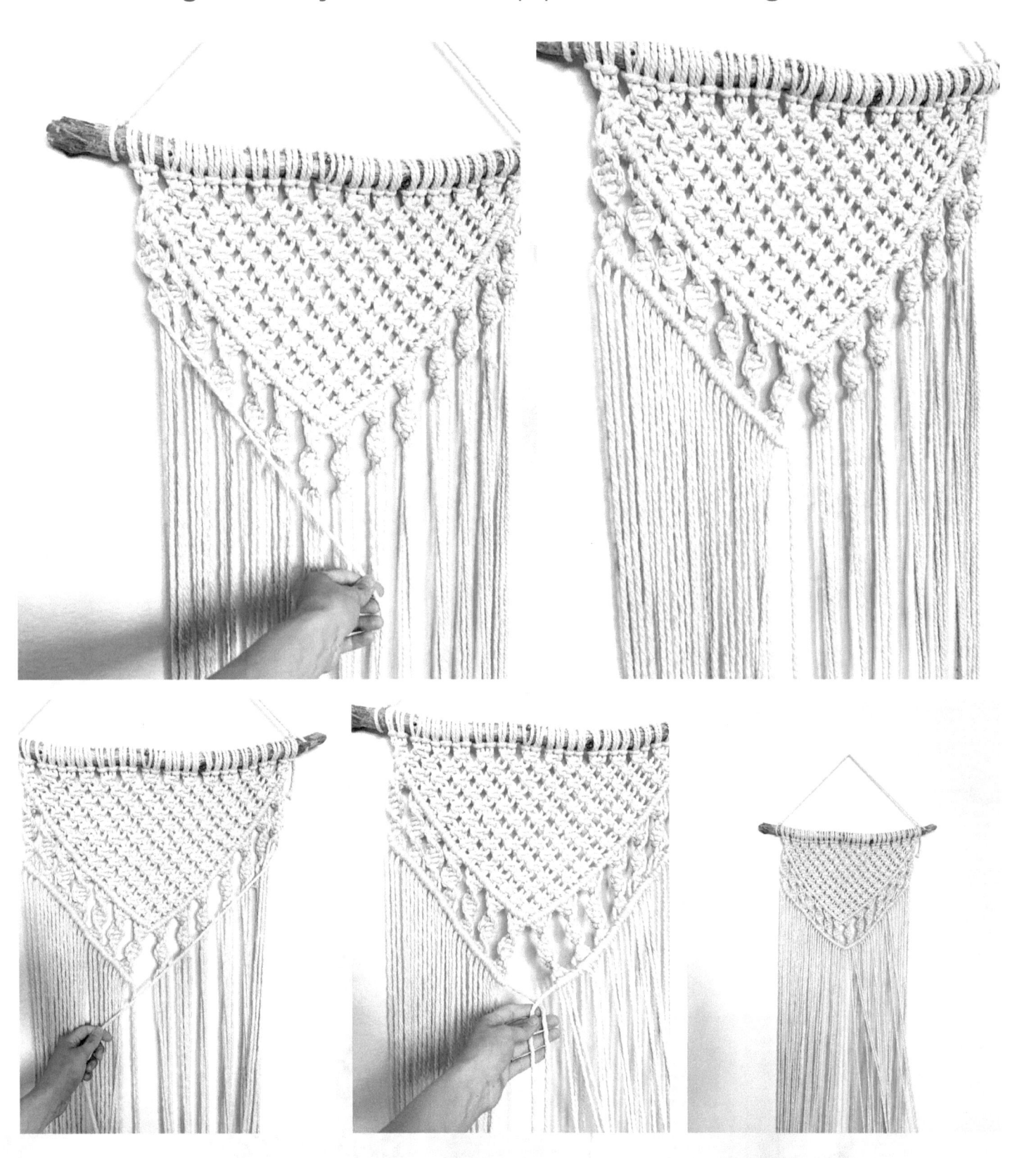

Photo Credits: (joyfulderivatives)

Step 5 - Finishing Off With Square Knots and Berry Knots

First, we will start by doing a row of square knots all along the bottom of the DHH from the previous step.

58 Finishing Off With Square Knots and Berry Knots

Photo Credits: (joyfulderivatives)

Now, we will make little berry knots!

Right in the middle, taking the two inner strands of cord from the two middle square knots, create a berry knot.

In the same way, using the next four, both to the right and left, make two more berry knots.

You should now have three berry knots in the middle of the triangle.

Photo Credits: (joyfulderivatives)

Close in the berry knots by making taking two strands from the middle berry and two from the left berry to create a square knot.

Repeat on the right side, using the other two strands from the middle berry and two from the right berry.

Make another square knot in the middle using those new square knot tails; this will continue the triangle shape of our macramé wall hanging.

Photo Credits: (joyfulderivatives)

Next, create the alternating square knot pattern we used for the top triangle, leaving the two unused cords at both the left and right ends.

Lastly, finish off the project by closing this section with DHH on either side. Make sure that the first knot is below the last row of square knots.
All that is left is to cut the tails to your desired length and hang your DIY macramé wall hanging!

There you have it!

62

For Home

DREAM CATCHER

Materials Required

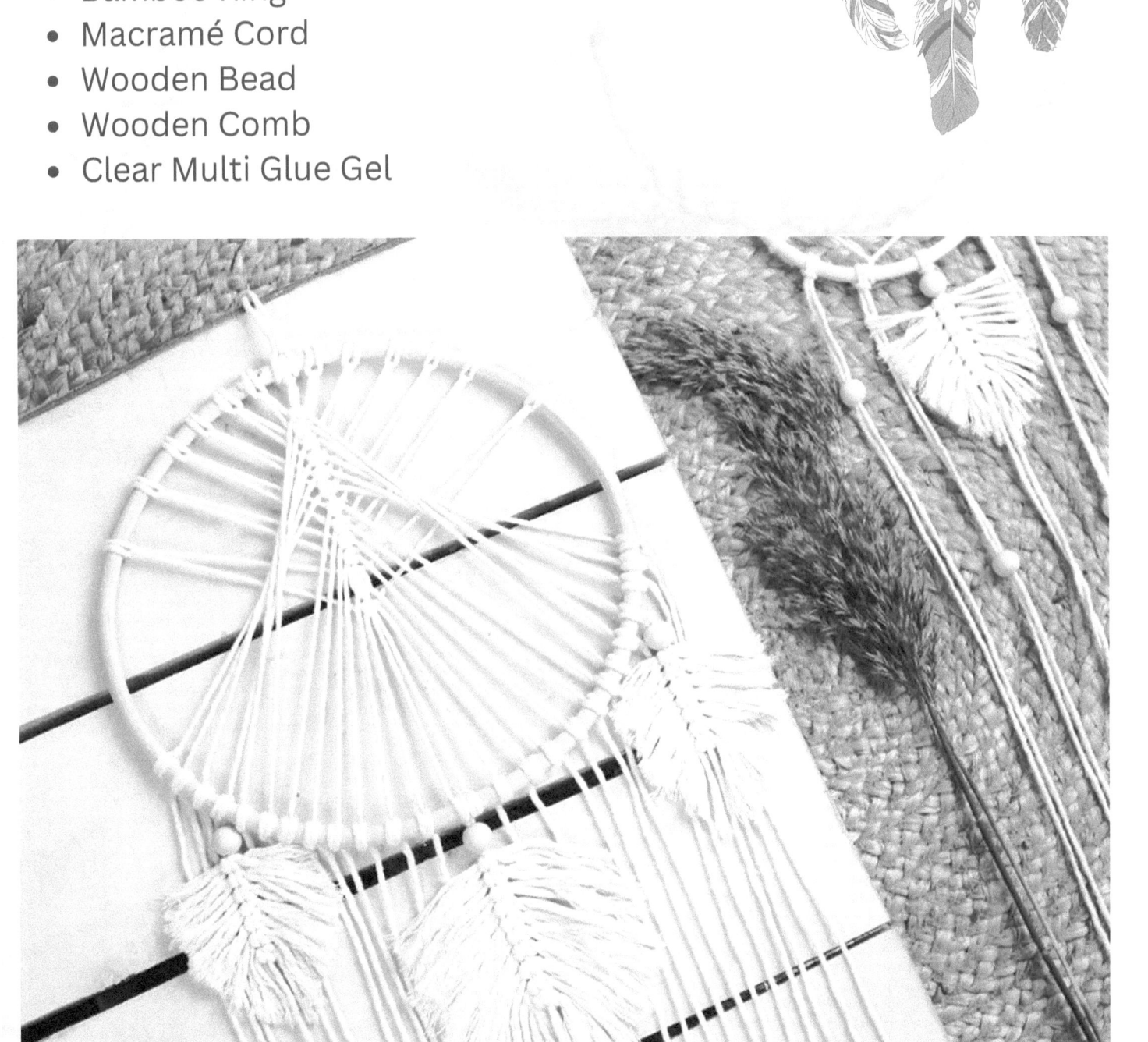

- Bamboo Ring
- Macramé Cord
- Wooden Bead
- Wooden Comb
- Clear Multi Glue Gel

Photo Credits: (Creativ Company)

Instructions

Step 1

Make a dream catcher with a stringent design by cutting 13 x 3 m pieces of cotton twine for a 25 cm diameter ring or cut 13 x 2 m pieces of cotton twine for a 20 cm diameter ring.

Tie a doubled-over piece of cotton twine onto the ring and secure it at the opposite side by twisting each cord around the ring and then tying a knot as shown in the photo. You will braid around this doubled over cord.

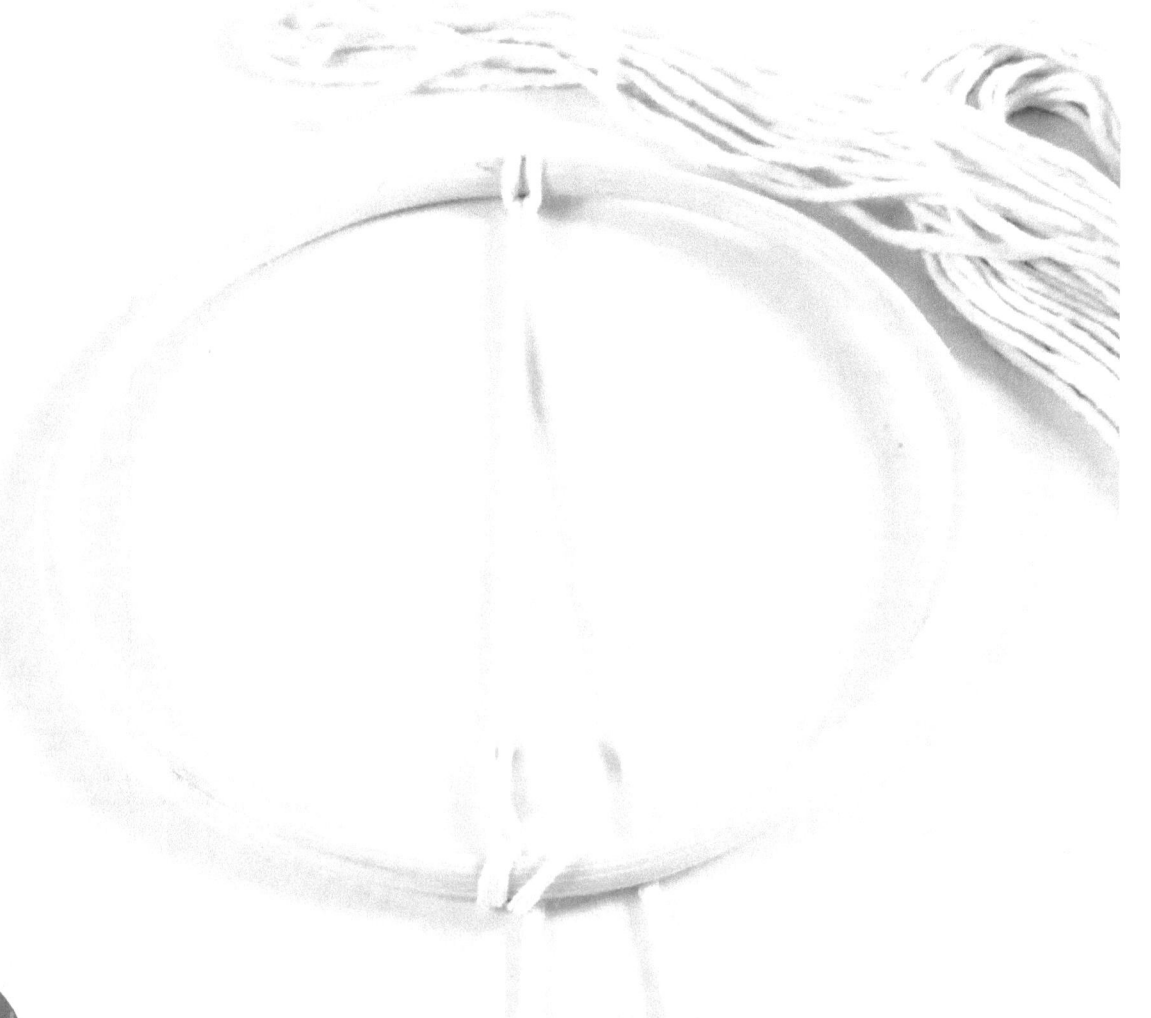

Photo Credits: (Creativ Company)

Step 2

Tie the doubled-over cords onto the top of the ring and feed the ends behind the previous cords. Tie a double knot with a cord from each side. Pull the cords downwards at an angle and tie them onto the sides of the ring as shown in the photo.

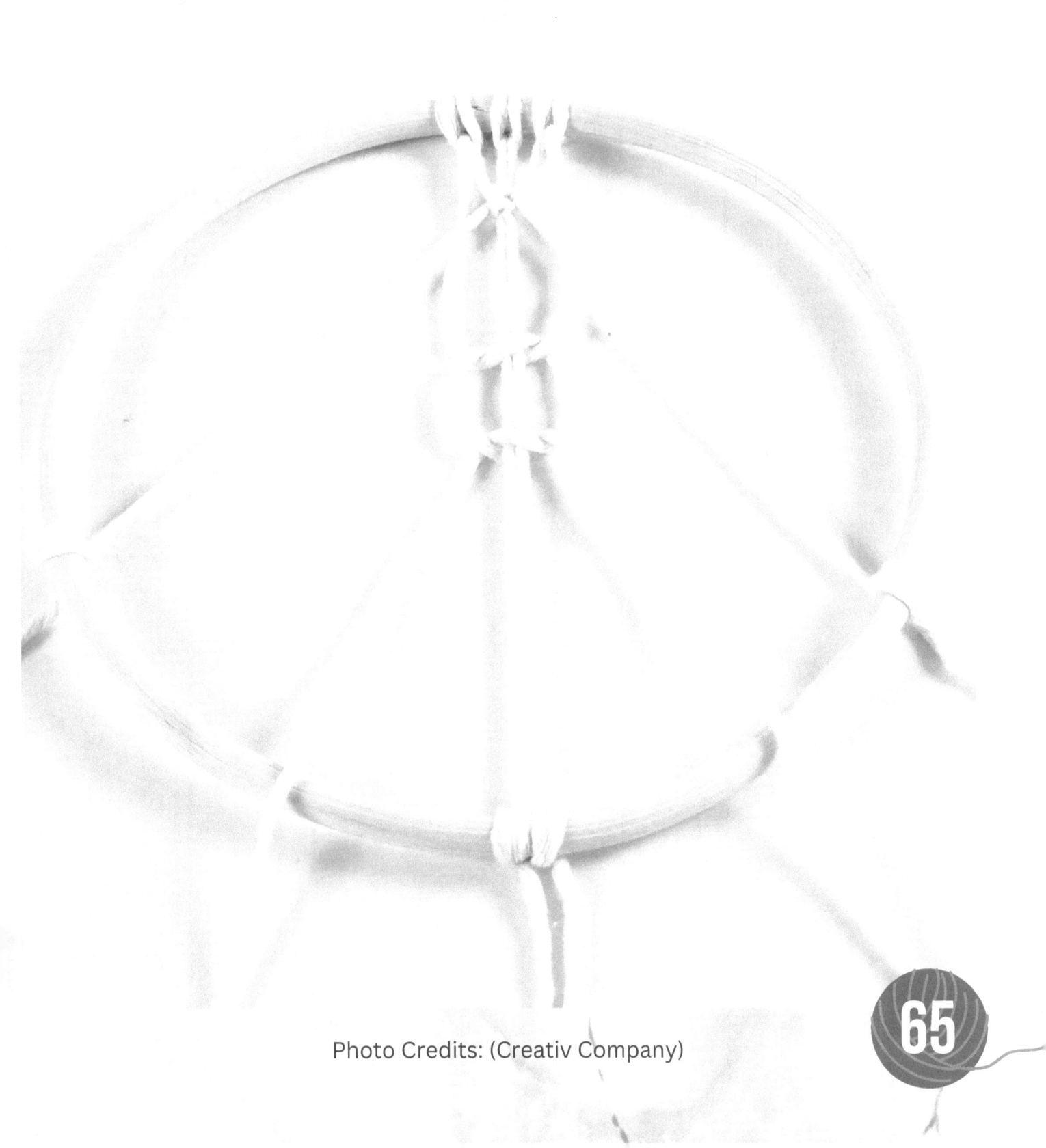

Photo Credits: (Creativ Company)

Step 3

Now, continue with all of the 12 pieces of cotton twine so that there are 6 cords on each side of the doubled-over twine in the middle.

Tie a double knot with the cords that cross behind the previous cords and then tie the ends onto the side of the ring right underneath each other as shown in the photo below.

Photo Credits: (Creativ Company)

Step 4

Twist the last cords straight down around the ring once and tie a knot. Then, adjust the knots so that the cords are equally spaced.

Photo Credits: (Creativ Company)

Step 5

Now, cut 20 x 14 cm pieces of cotton twine for the large leaf and double them over and then, tie them onto one of the middle cords in pairs as shown in the photo below.

For each of the two small leaves cut 14 x 10 cm pieces of cotton twine and make leaves around the two outer cords following the same procedure.

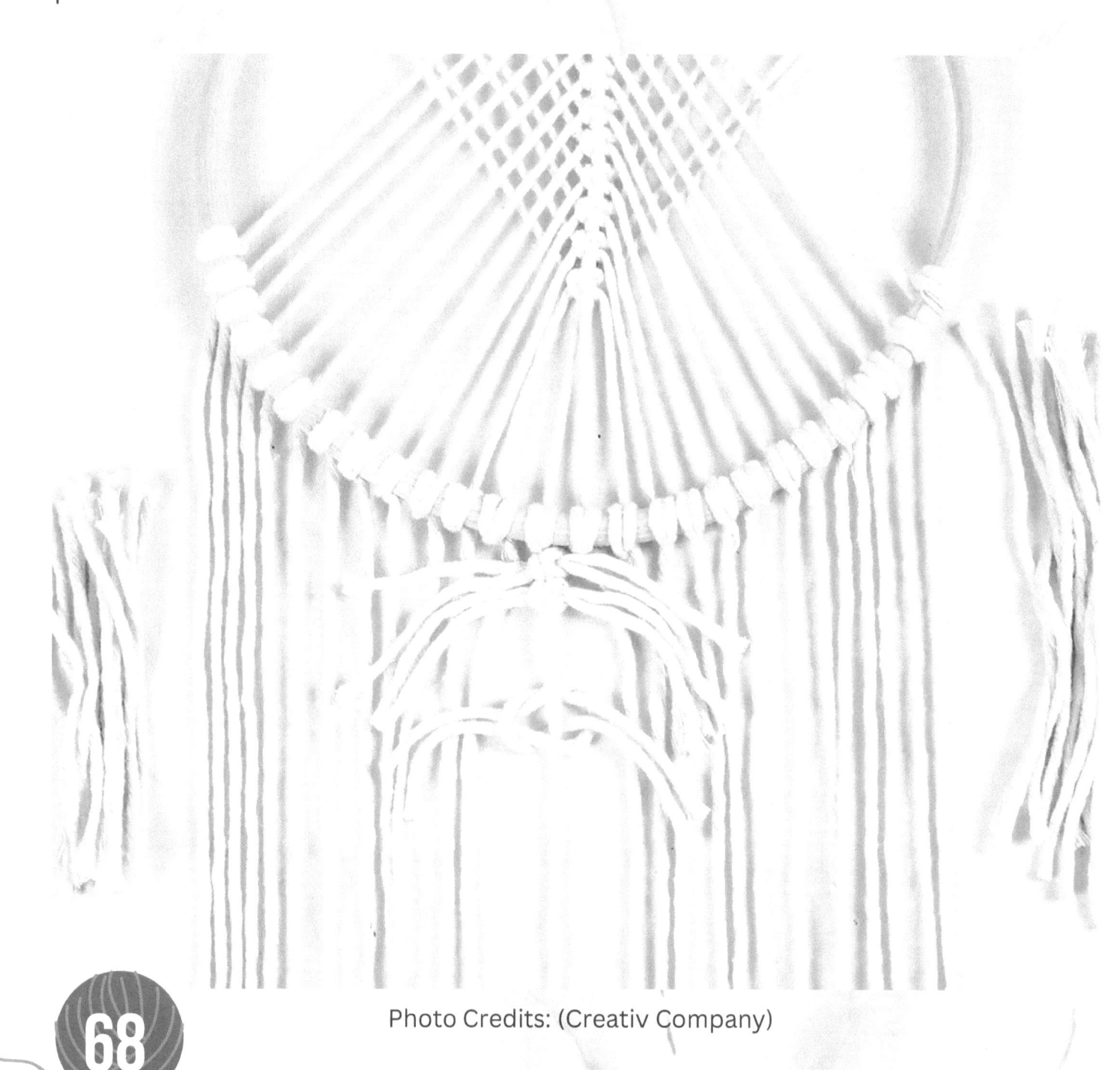

Photo Credits: (Creativ Company)

Step 6

Unravel the cotton twine with a comb. Trim into a leaf shape using a pair of scissors. A tip: Make the cotton twine leaves wet and put them under pressure to get a beautiful shape.

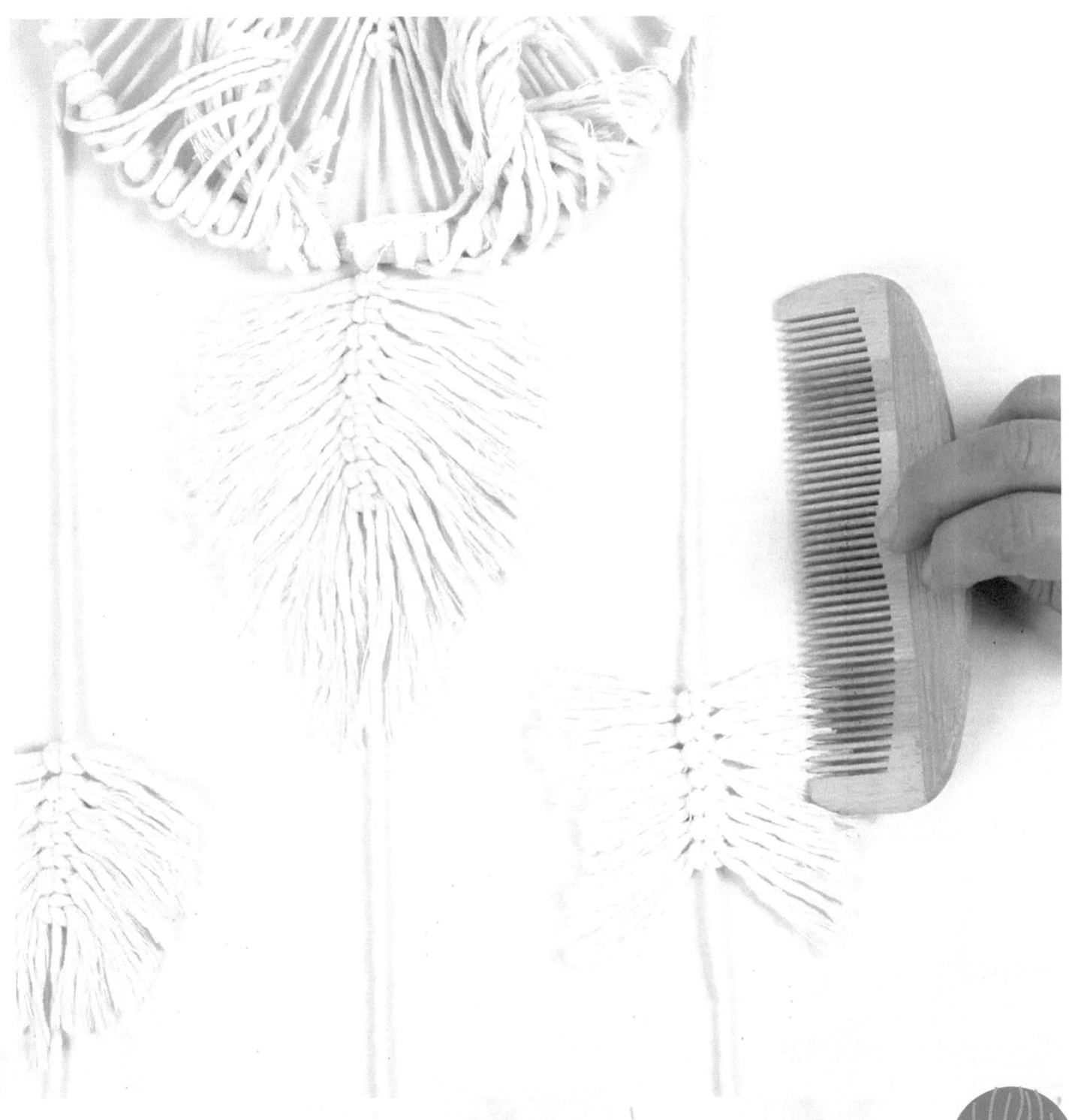

Photo Credits: (Creativ Company)

Step 7

Thread wooden beads onto the long pieces of cotton twine which are hanging down from the dream catcher.

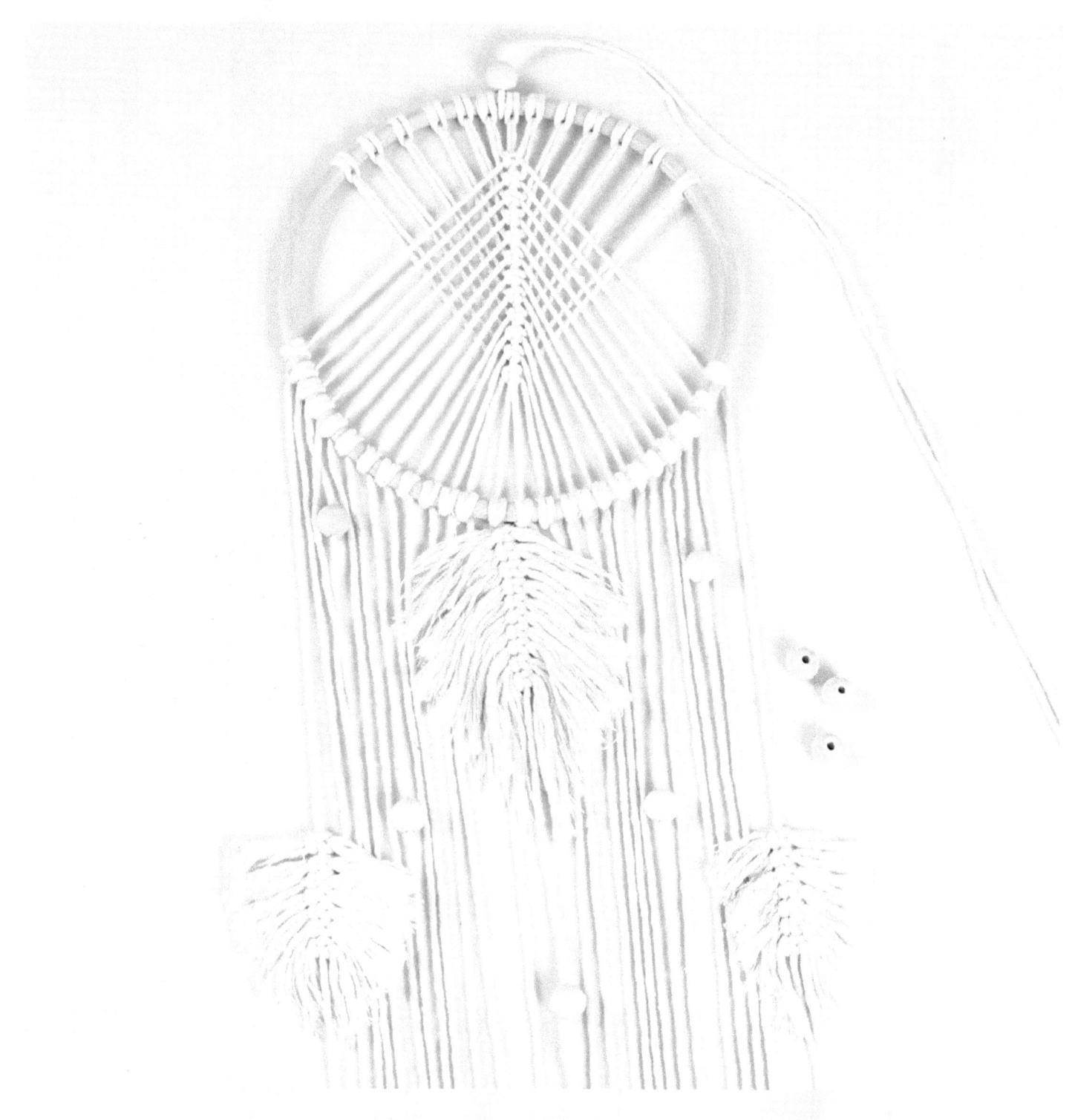

Photo Credits: (Creativ Company)

Step 8

Trim the long pieces of cotton twine into a pointed shape at your chosen length. Unravel the lowest 5 cm with a comb.

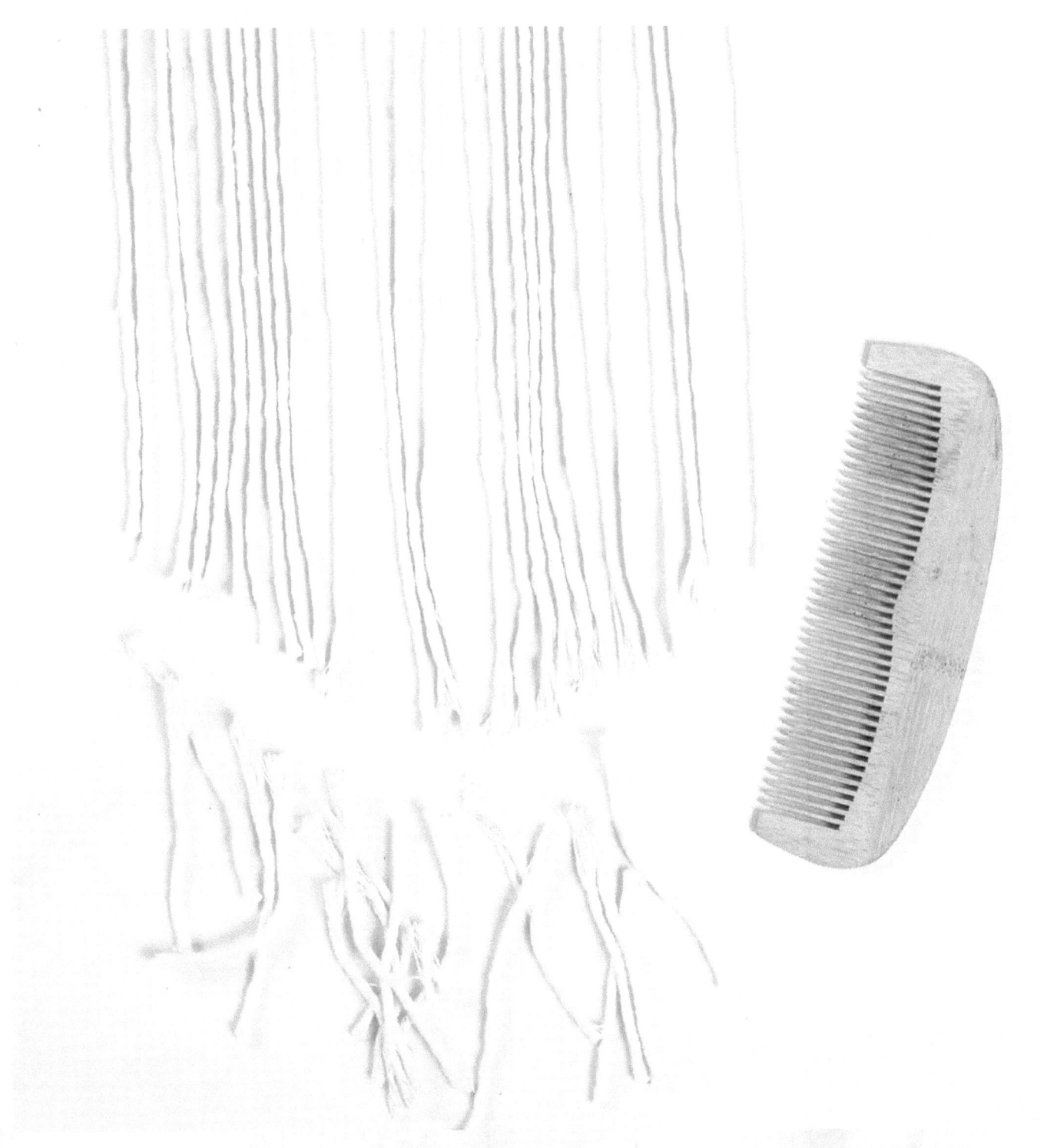

Photo Credits: (Creativ Company)

Step 9

Make a dream catcher with a classic design by cutting a 1 x 2.5 m piece of cotton twine for a 15 cm diameter ring. Divide the ring into 8 sections, 5.5-6 cm long and mark each with a pencil.

Tie the cotton twine onto one of the pencil marks and twist the twine around the ring. Cross in front of the twine before securing the twine onto the ring at the next pencil mark as shown in the photo.

Photo Credits: (Creativ Company)

Step 10

Continue wrapping the twine tightly around the middle of the next piece of cotton twine all the way around and cross in before the next round. Continue until the pattern reaches the middle of the ring.

Tighten as you go along and hold onto the last knot with your index finger and thumb whilst making the next knot. Finish by making a knot on either side of a wooden bead. Apply a small blob of glue onto the very first knot and the last knot. Trim the twine closely.

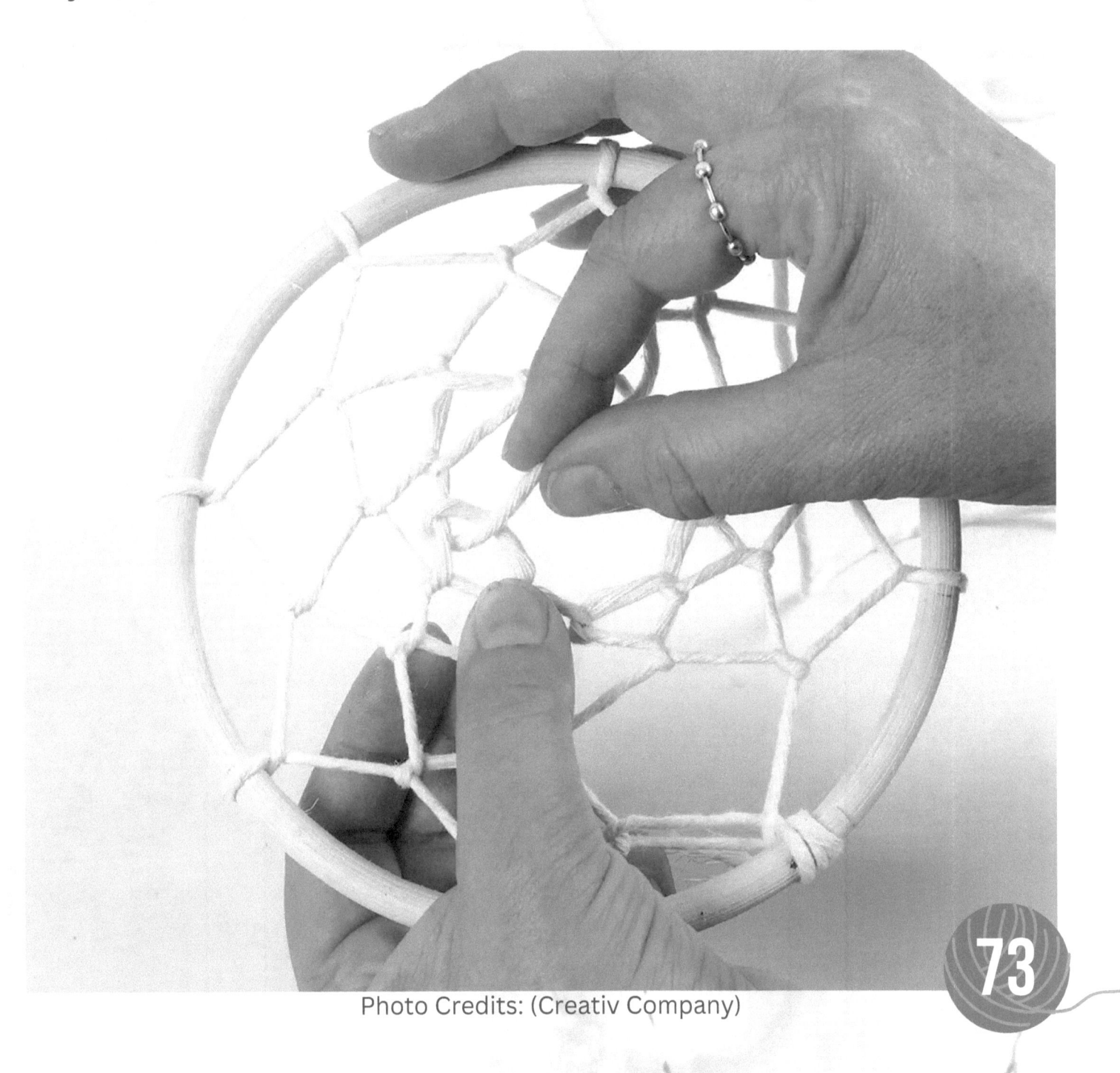

Photo Credits: (Creativ Company)

Step 11

Here is a 15 cm diameter ring with a classic dream catcher pattern.

Photo Credits: (Creativ Company)

For Home

EASY WALL HANGING

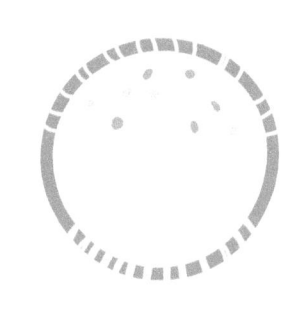

Materials Required

- Cotton Macramé Cording
- Hoop in any size you want
- Wooden beads
- Faux Flowers (optional – I added some to make it a bit more whimsical and girly)

Photo Credits: (Decor Hint)

75

Instructions

Step 1

Start by cutting equal lengths of macramé cord. It doesn't have to be perfect – I made mine about 14 inches each, give or take.

Step 2

Fold each cord in half and tie each onto the hoop using a lark's head knot.

Step 3

I tied exactly 28 lark's head knots onto the hoop. You can do more or less depending on how wide you want it to be.

Step 4

Taking two adjacent macramé cords at a time, string the wooden beads on, spacing them out as you see fit. I tried one cord and the beads would slip off. Two cords were perfect, although it does take some finesse to string them through the beads.

Step 5

Evenly cut the bottom so it's nice and straight.

Step 6

Optional – take a collection of beautiful faux flowers and greens and attach them to your hoop on one of the sides. I used floral tape to attach them and I found working on the back side of the hoop to be the easiest. That's it!

For Home

MACRAMÉ CHANDELIER

Materials Required

- Lampshade
- Scissors
- 35M of Cotton Rope
- Iron

Photo Credits: (Collective Gen)

Instructions

For this project we will have to buy 35 metres of 0.5 cm cotton, three strand rope (40 yards of 3/8 inch rope), which we will then separate into three strands for a softer feel.

This, therefore will give us 105m of rope (114 yards of 3/8 rope). If you don't use three strand rope or don't want to unravel it, you'll need to buy 105m instead of the 35m. We will end up with a macramé chandelier that is 25cm in length for the macramé part and 20cm in length for the tassel part (that's 10 inches for the macramé and 8 inches for the tassel).

Step 1

We will deconstruct a cheap lampshade for the base that measured about 30 cm in diameter (12 inches). Remove the covering so the wire is left over. Here in this project, we ended up just using the top wire frame and the light holder, and didn't use the bottom one.

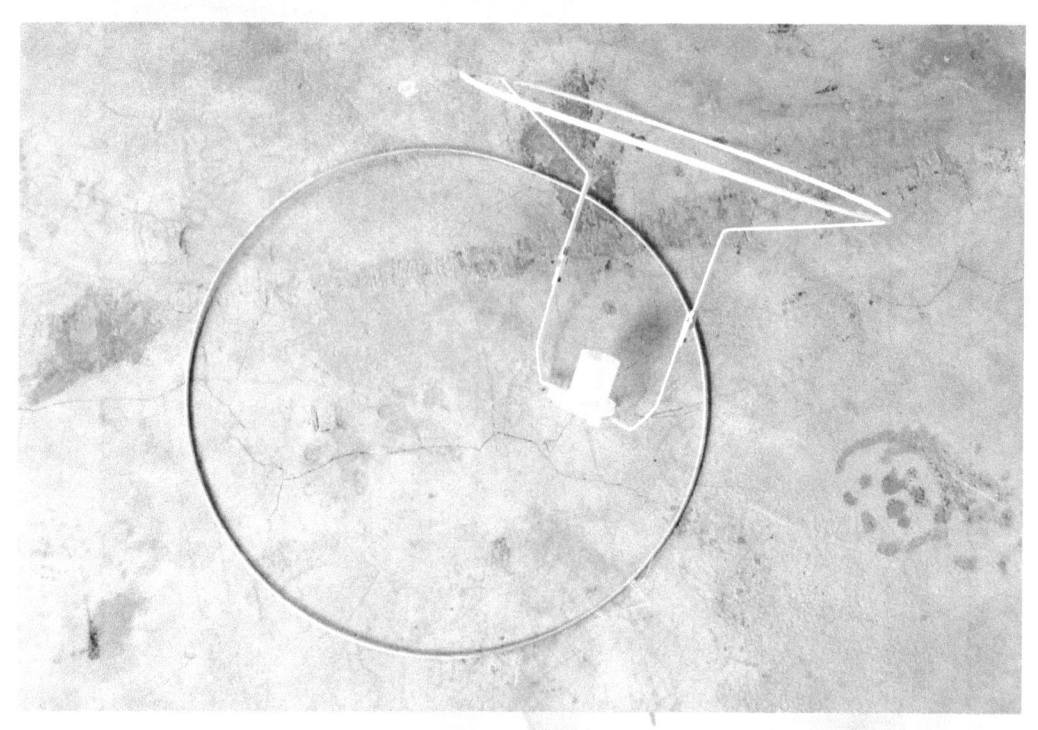

Step 2

First, cut your rope to size, our pieces were 3 metres per piece or 118 inches, and then unravel it into three strands. FYI The formula for working out rope length is length of the final woven chandelier times 6, since you'll be folding the pieces in half before knotting them to the lampshade base.

Step 3

To get that gorgeous soft tassel look, we will unravel the rope and then iron it to make it straighter.

Step 4

Fold your separated pieces of rope in half before tying them to the lampshade base using a reverse larks head knot as shown below.

Step 5

Begin the first row on the chandelier by tying half knots.

Photo Credits: (Collective Gen)

Step 6

Measure down 1" from the top row of knots, and begin knotting the first row of square knots.

Step 7

After completing the first row, measure down 1" again and begin knotting the second row of square knots, using alternating strands from the previous row.

Step 8

The next row will be two rows of half knots without any space in between, which creates a thick woven border at the bottom.

Step 9

Then we're going to do some twisting half knots. There isn't any trick to doing this, since the knots will begin twisting on their own once you keep knotting. We did 15 half knots for each, and we ended up with 4" long twisted pieces.

Step 10

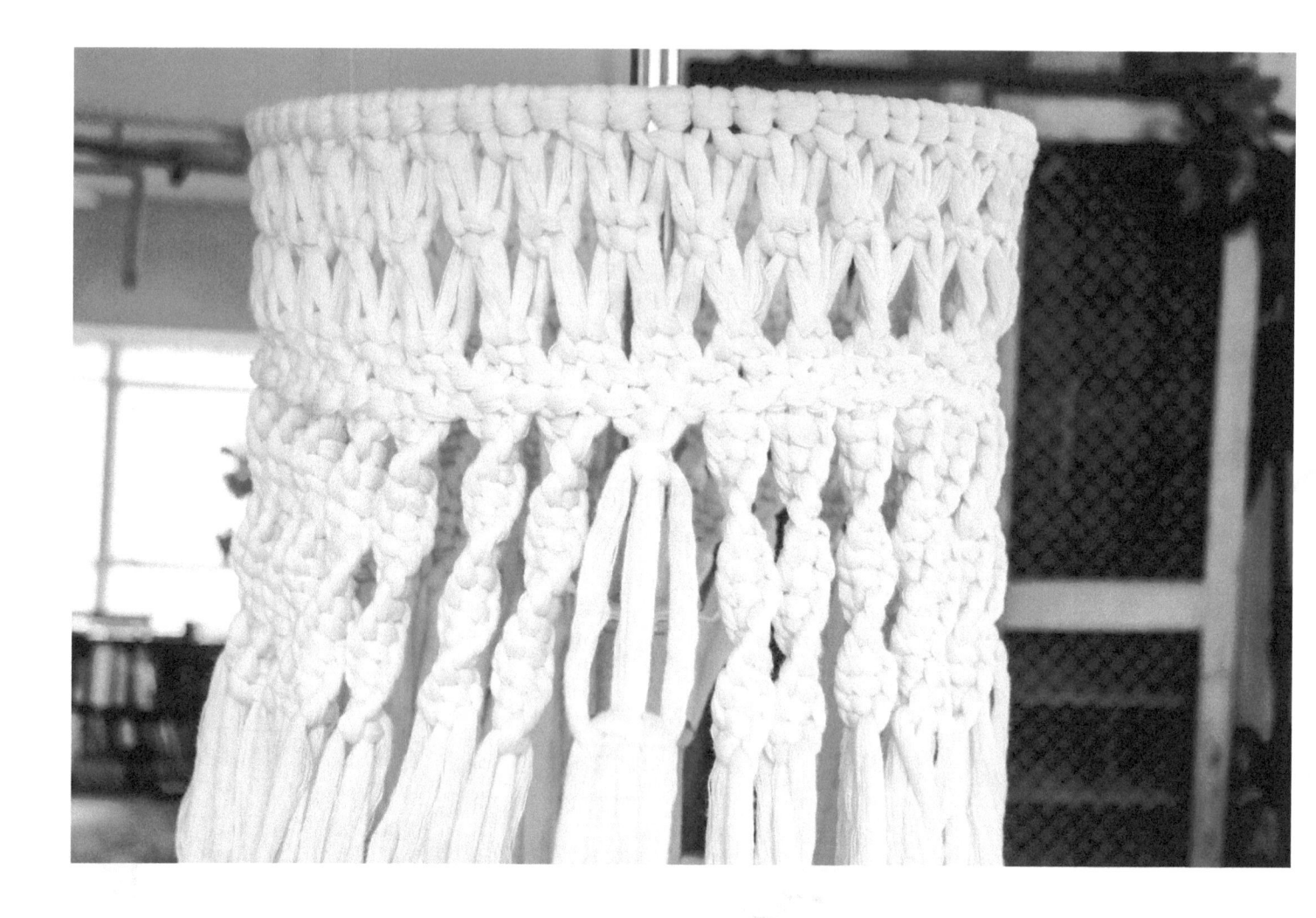

Measure the twisted pieces, and adjust them until the lengths are the same, then we're going to do two more rows of half knots to weave a thick border at the bottom.

Step 11

This is what the bottom of the chandelier will look like after weaving the bottom border.

Step 12

The final step is to measure the ideal length for the tassels and snip off the excess rope.

and the Chandelier is READYyy!!!

86

For Home

PILLOW COVER

Materials Required

- Tape measure
- pair of scissors
- macramé cords
- 20 in. x 20 in. pillow cover
- stick or dowel

Photo Credits: (DIY Projects)

Instructions

Step 1 - Cut the Macramé Cord

Cut down 16 stands of your macramé cord worth 12 feet long. This should be a sufficient length to cover your entire pillow insert.

Photo Credits: (DIY Projects)

Step 2 - Thread your Cords Using a Reverse Lark's Head Knot

Next, take your dowel and use a lark's head knot to attach your cords to it.

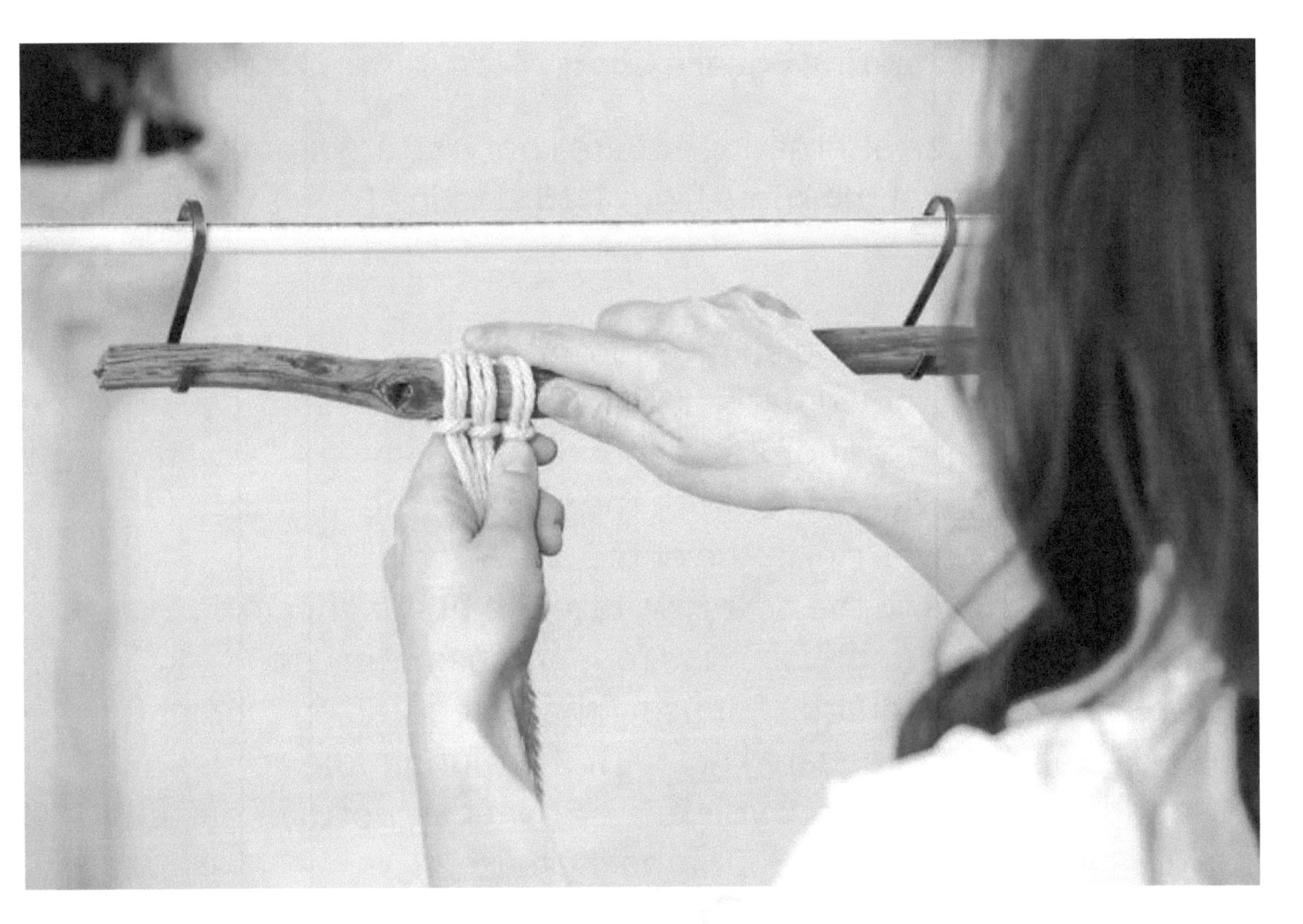

Photo Credits: (DIY Projects)

Step 3 - Make a Row of Square Knots

Now that you've threaded your cords into your dowel, it's time to start your first row of square knots. Continue taking two Lark's head knots at a time (for a total of four strands) until you have 16 square knots.

Step 4 - Make Alternating Square Knots

Continue on with an alternating square knot pattern. For easier reference, we'll label the knots from 1-16 starting from the leftmost square knot.

1. Take square knot 1 and square knot 2.
2. Make a square knot with the four macramé cords in the middle.
3. Move on to square knot 2 and square knot 3.
4. Make another square knot with the cords in the middle.
5. Continue until you finish the entire row.
6. Once you move to the next row, take the first eight cords.
7. Create a square knot using the four cords on the left.
8. Create another square knot using the four cords on the right.
9. Make yet another square knot with the four middle cords.
10. Continue steps 7-9 until you reach 20 inches worth of pattern. You can track this with your tape measure.

Step 5 - Close with a Double Half Hitch

Now that you're done with the pattern, it's time to close this off with a double half hitch knot.

Step 6 - Cut Off the Excess Cord

Cut off the excess cords, but leave around 5 inches worth of fringe behind. Once you're done, detach the pattern from your dowel.

Step 7 - Attach Pattern to your Pillow Cover

With your pattern done, you can then attach it to your pillow cover. You can either sew in the pattern by hand or use a sewing machine to get the job done faster.

91

For Planters

PLANT HANGER

Materials Required

- 10 yards of cording, twine, or paracord
- 1-1/4-inch metal ring or key ring
- 6-inch-tall ceramic planter

Photo Credits: (Adam Albright)

We used a 6-inch-tall pot for our macramé hanger, but you can customize the overall size to fit your planter of choice. When selecting a pot, consider how you'll deal with drainage. Most plants prefer pots with a drainage hole so the soil doesn't remain overly wet, but if you water a hanging plant with a hole in the bottom, it'll drain straight onto your floor. Plan to move your plant to the sink each time you water, or use a cachepot (a decorative exterior container that can disguise a basic plastic pot) to catch drainage. If you opt for a pot with no drainage hole, be extra careful not to over-water your plant.

Instructions

Step 1 - Tie strands to ring

Cut four 90-inch-long cording strands and lay them together in a group. Thread all the strands through the metal ring, and tie the centers of the strands to the ring. Tighten and even out the strands as needed.

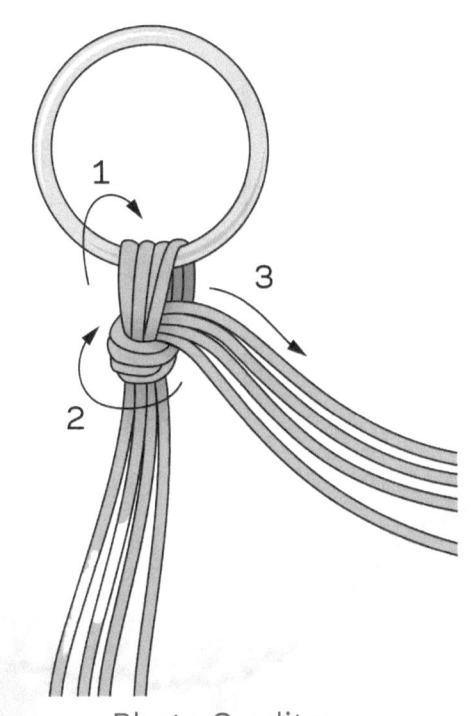

Photo Credits:
(ILLUSTRATION BY LIZ GORDON)

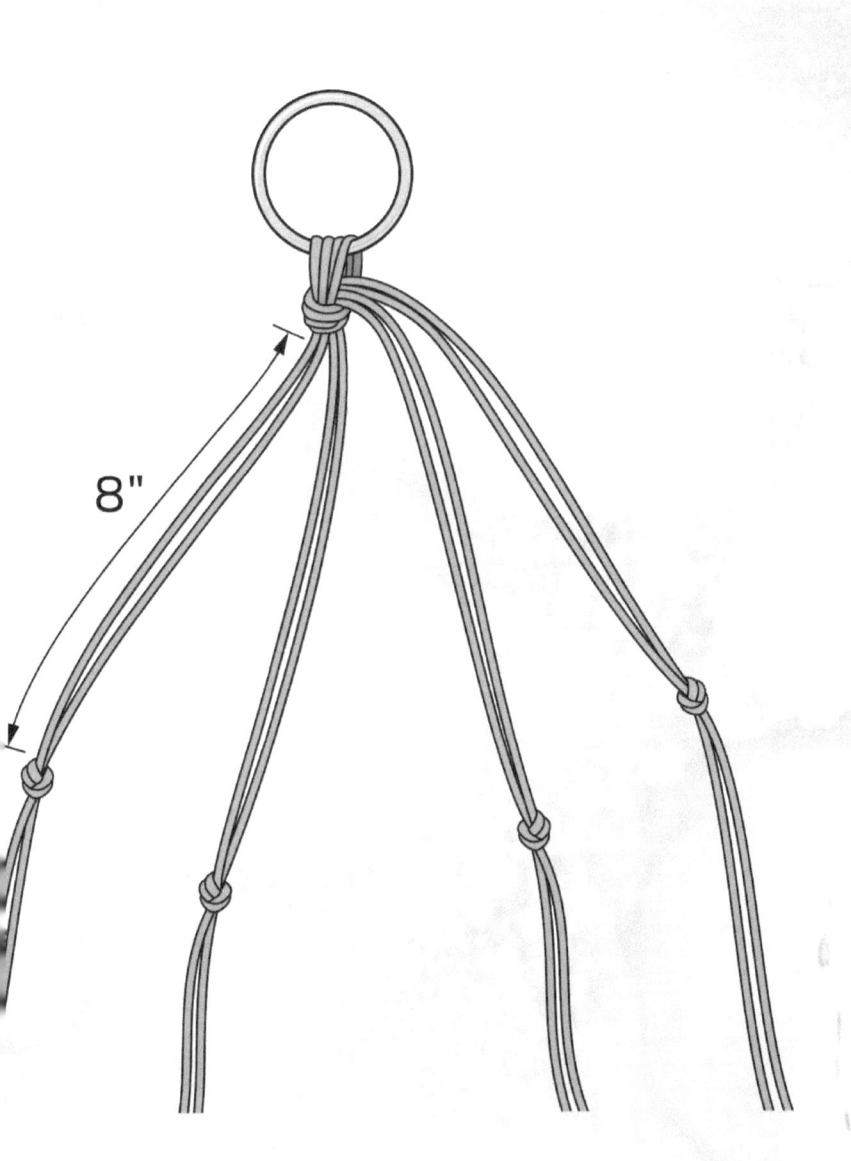

Step 2 - Section off strands

Split the strands into four sections of two strands each. Tie each section with an overhand knot approximately 8 inches below the top knot. Be sure to pull the strands tight to avoid uneven lengths between knots.

Photo Credits:
(ILLUSTRATION BY LIZ GORDON)

Step 3 - Split tails and tie

Split the tails below each knot and join them with tails from adjacent knots. Secure the strands with an overhand knot approximately 3 to 4 inches below the knots from Step 2. Measurements don't need to be exact but place the knots at similar lengths for a neat finish.

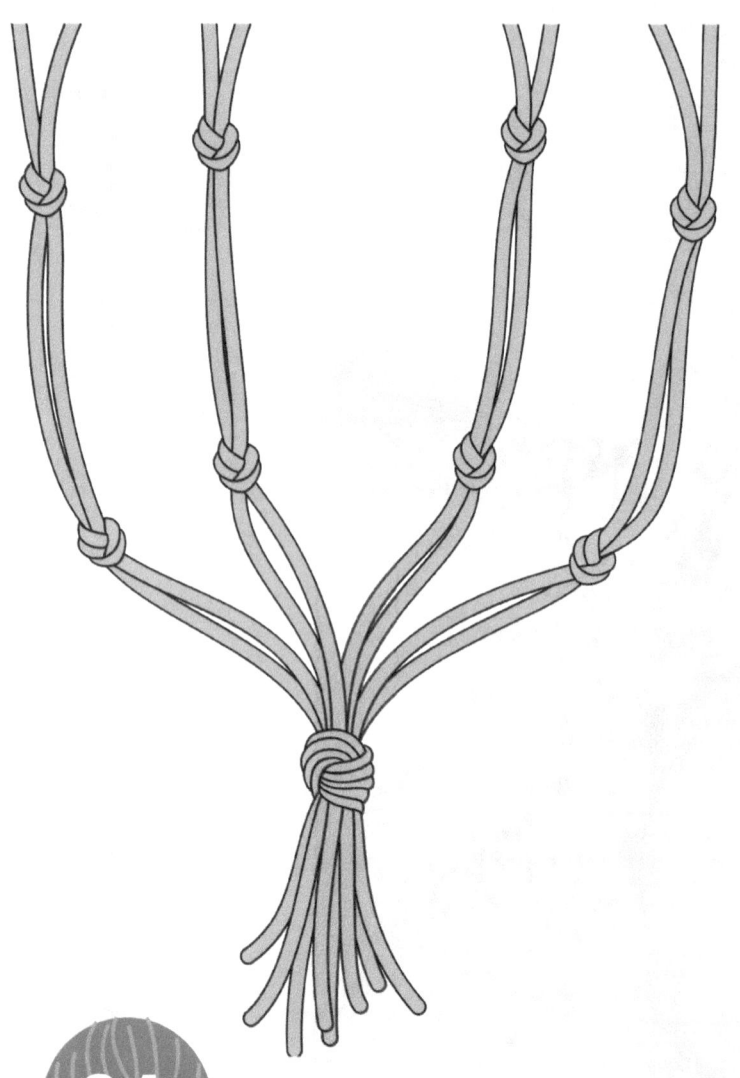

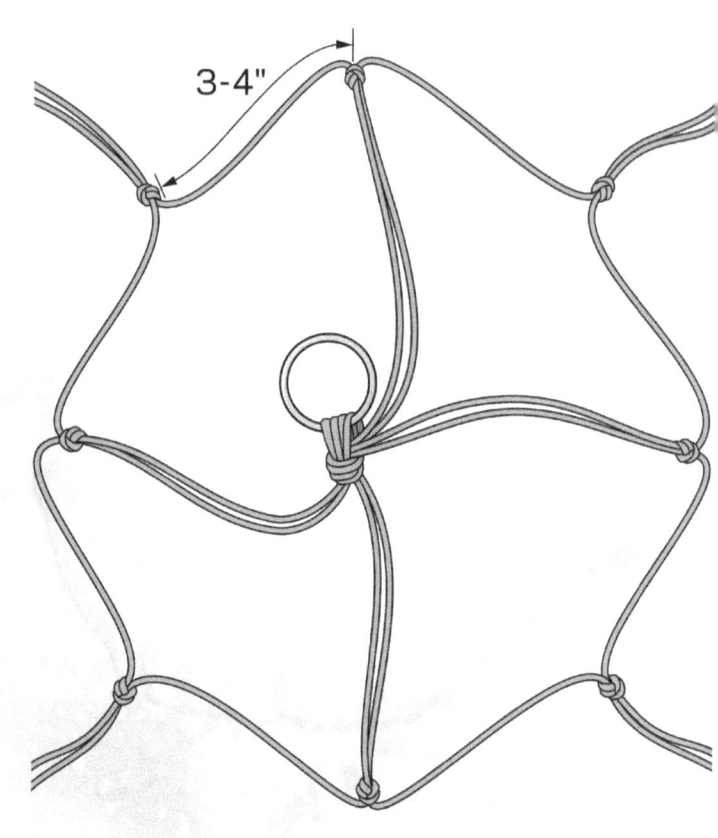

Photo Credits:
(ILLUSTRATION BY LIZ GORDON)

Step 4 - Tie all tails together

Group all the tails together and knot them with a large overhand knot. This will hold the planter in place, so make sure the knot is sturdy. Trim the tails to your desired length based on design preference.

Photo Credits:
(ILLUSTRATION BY LIZ GORDON)

Step 5 - Insert plant and hang

Insert the planter into your macramé hanger. Install a ceiling hook that's designed to support the weight of the potted plant. Make sure to choose a spot that receives enough light for your plant, and secure the hook into a stud or an anchor so it doesn't pull out of the ceiling. Place the top ring over the ceiling hook to hang.

Photo Credits: (Adam Albright)

FEATHER ORNAMENT

For Holydays

Materials Required

- 4 mm 3 strand twisted cotton
(1 piece @ 16" long – 16 pieces @ 7" long)
- Cinnamon stick
- Twine for hanger
- Felt
- Hot glue gun
- Cork board or macramé board
- T-pins
- Sharp scissors

Photo Credits: (Marching North)

Instructions

Step 1

First, take a cinnamon stick and fold the long piece of cord in half and attach it to the stick with a lark's head knot.

Photo Credits: (Marching North)

Step 2

Now, you're going to take one of the short pieces and fold it in half.

Hold it perpendicular to the long center cord, and put the looped end under the center cords with the loop pointing to the left.

Then grab another short piece and you are going to lay it on top of the first piece, with the ends facing in the opposite direction. The loop will be facing right.

Basically, you'll have a sandwich situation going on with the right short piece on the bottom, the center cords in the middle, and the left short cord on the top.

Then, thread the ends of each short cord through the loop of the opposite cord, and pull the ends to tighten it up.

Step 3

Now, repeat the same process for the remaining short cords.

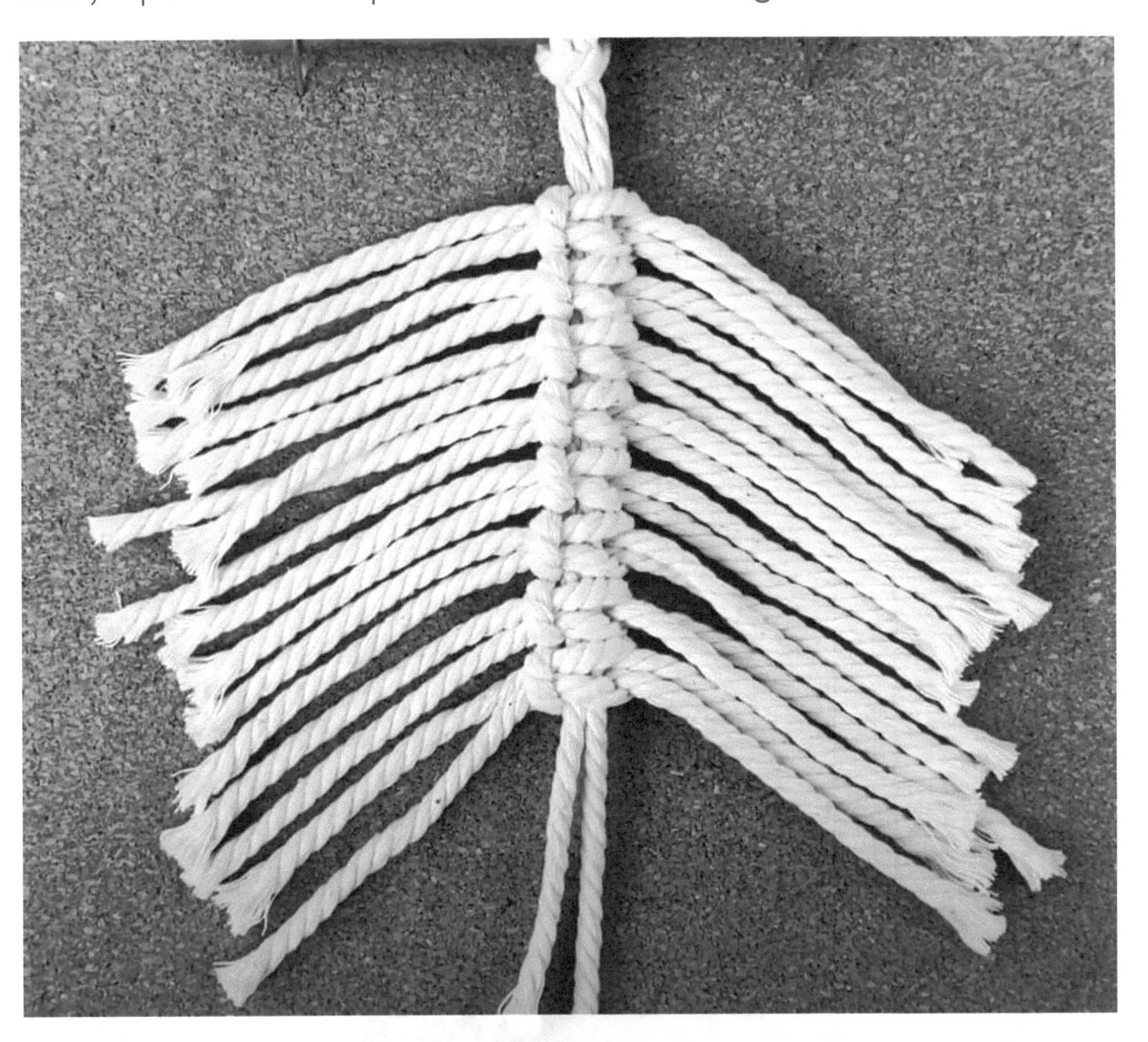

Step 4

Grab your macramé brush or comb, and brush out the fringe really well on both sides.

Step 5

Now we're going to cut a small piece of felt to go on the back of the feather to help hold it's shape. This is optional, but it really helps keep your ornament looking good for years to come.

Step 6

You want to make sure the felt piece isn't going to show from the front. I eyeballed mine and just trimmed it down until it was how I wanted it to look.

Make sure the feather is neatly brushed, and use your hot glue gun to attach the felt to the back of your feather.

Now you can flip your ornament back over and cut the edges to shape the feather. Add a small piece of jute or twine to the top of the ornament to make a hanger and you're done!

Photo Credits: (Marching North)

For Holydays

BOHO ORNAMENT

Materials Required

- 3 mm single strand cotton string
(6 pieces @ 24" long)
(1 piece @ approx. 8" long for hanger)
- 2" wood ring
- Cork board or macramé board
- T-pins
- Sharp scissors

Photo Credits: (Marching North)

102

Instructions

Step 1

Attach the six pieces of cord to the wooden ring with lark's head knots. Then pin or tape it down to your workspace to hold it while you knot.

Photo Credits: (Marching North)

Step 2

Tie three square knots going across. Then, tie two more square knots, alternating from the first row. Tie one last square knot in the center.

104

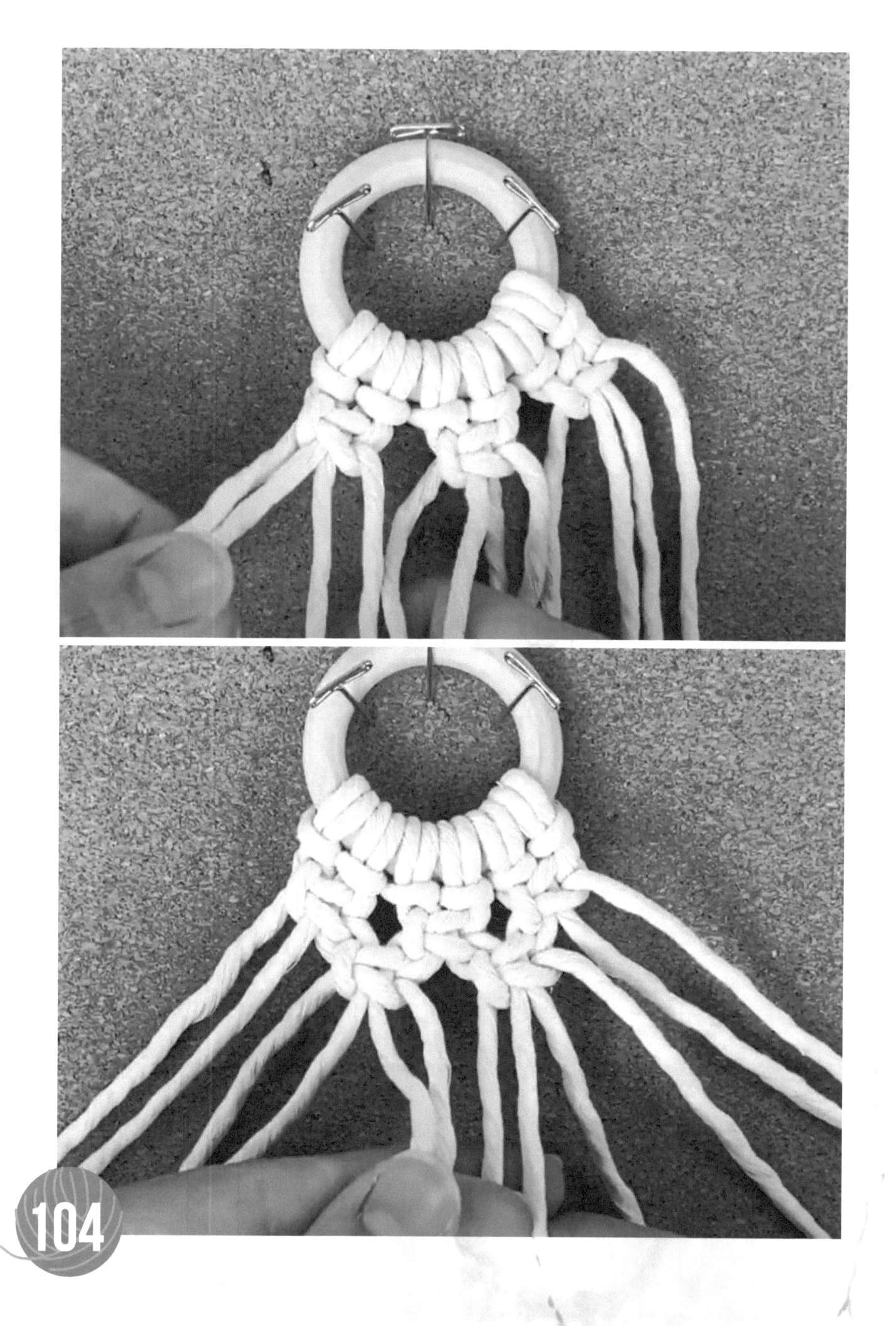

Step 3

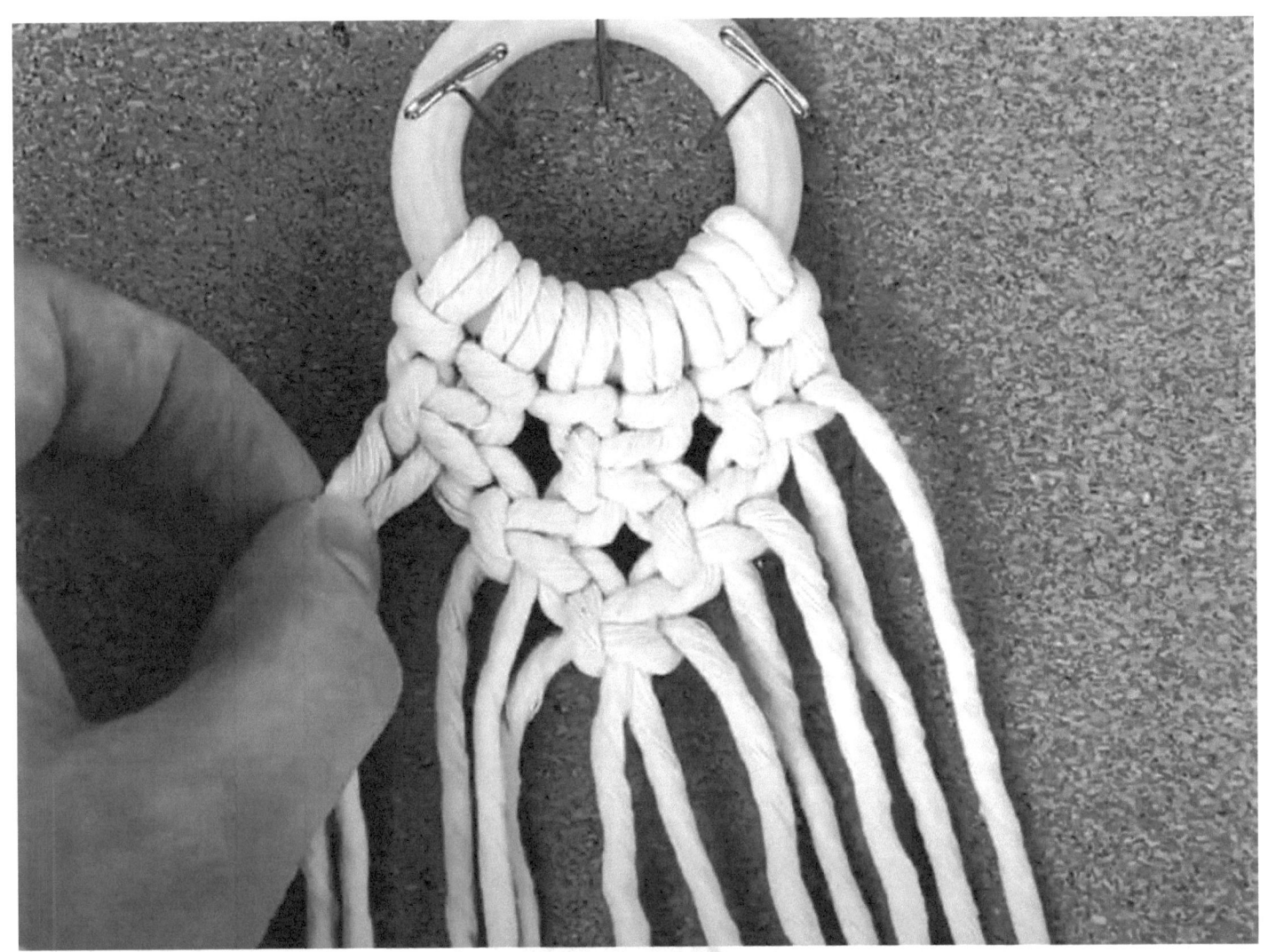

Use the far left cord as the filler cord and tie 5 DHH knots going down and to the right.

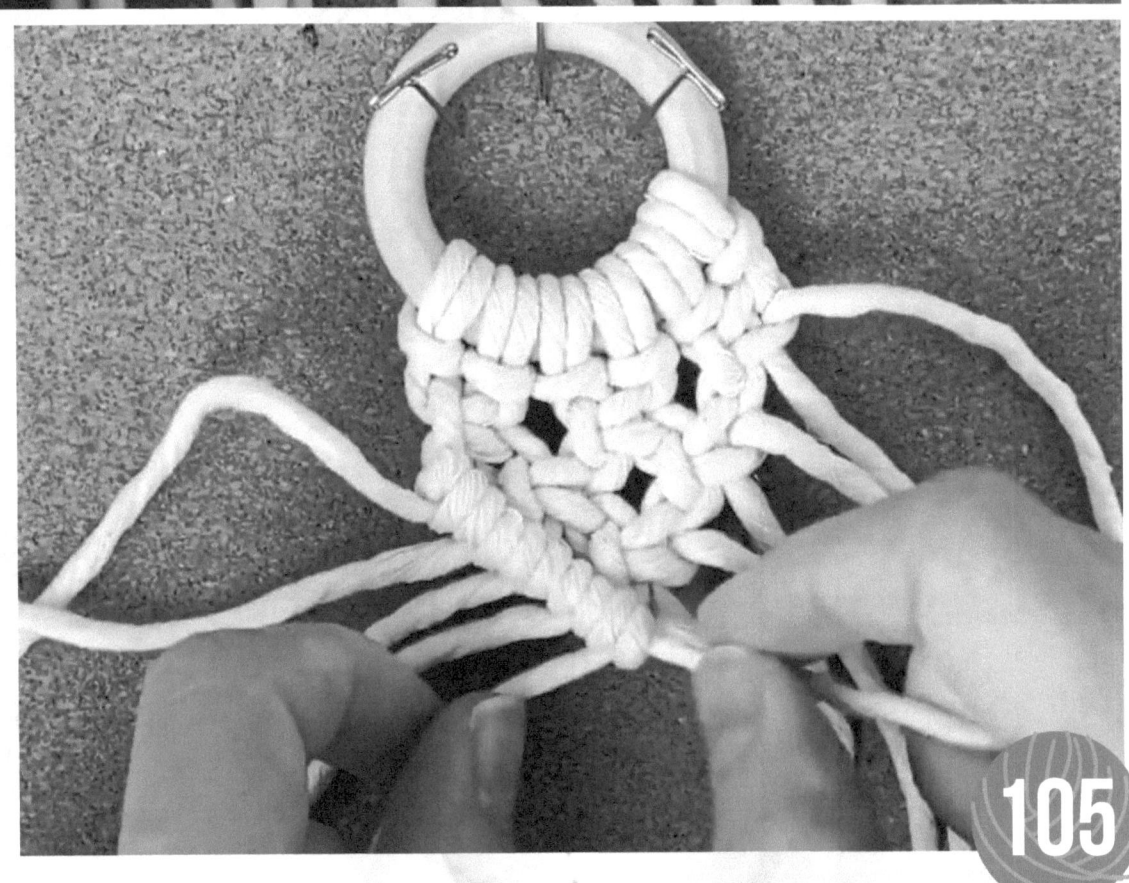

Step 4

Use the far right cord as the filler cord and tie six double half hitch knots going down and to the left. The last knot will connect the two sides.

Step 5

Attach the hanging cord to the top of the ring with a lark's head knot. Thread the wooden bead onto the hanging cord at the top. I used a large eye needle and threaded one piece through at a time.

107

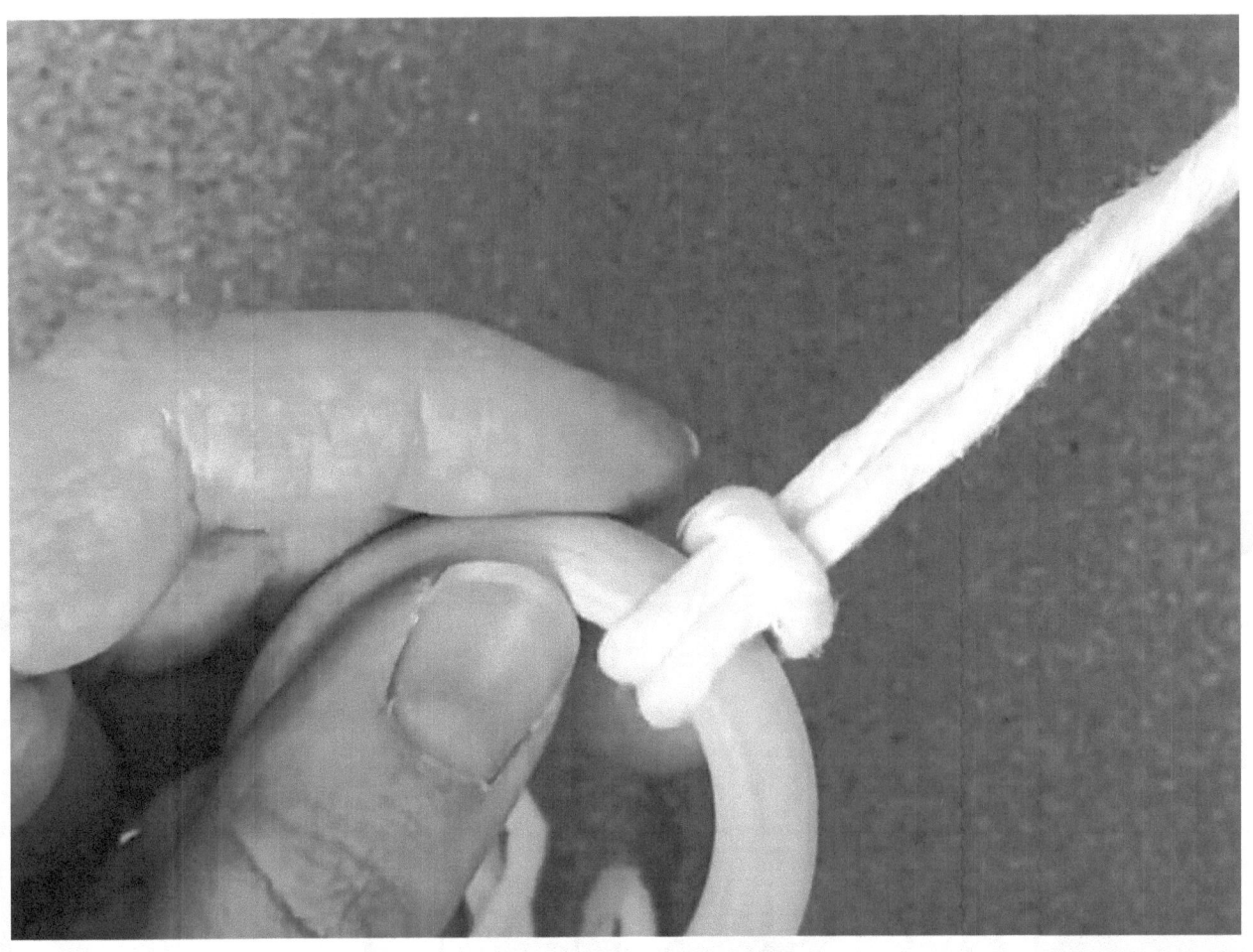

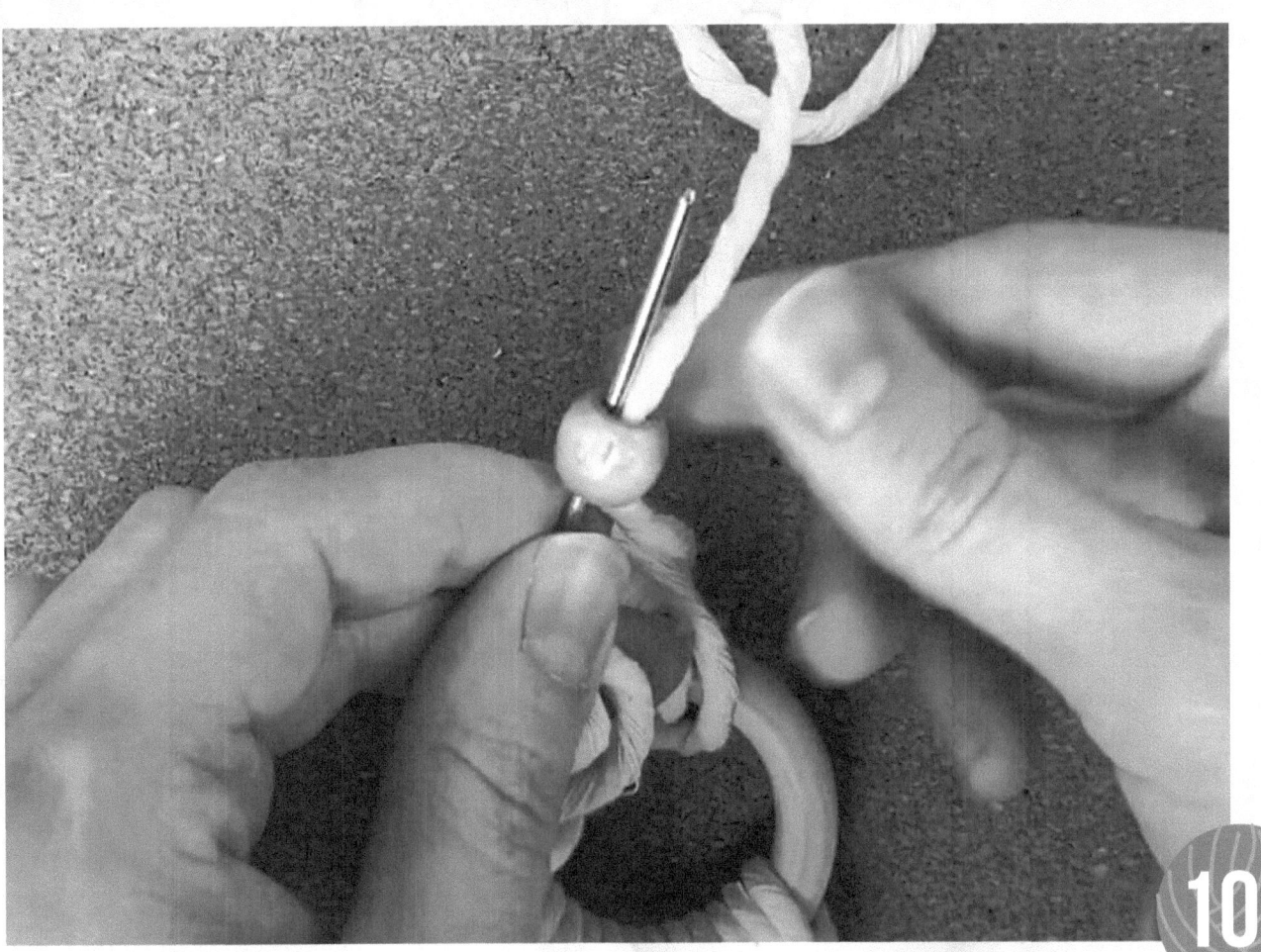

Step 6

Tie an overhand knot a couple of inches above the bead and trim off the excess cord to make the hanging loop.

And finally, cut the fringe in the shape you want, brush it out, and give it a final trim.

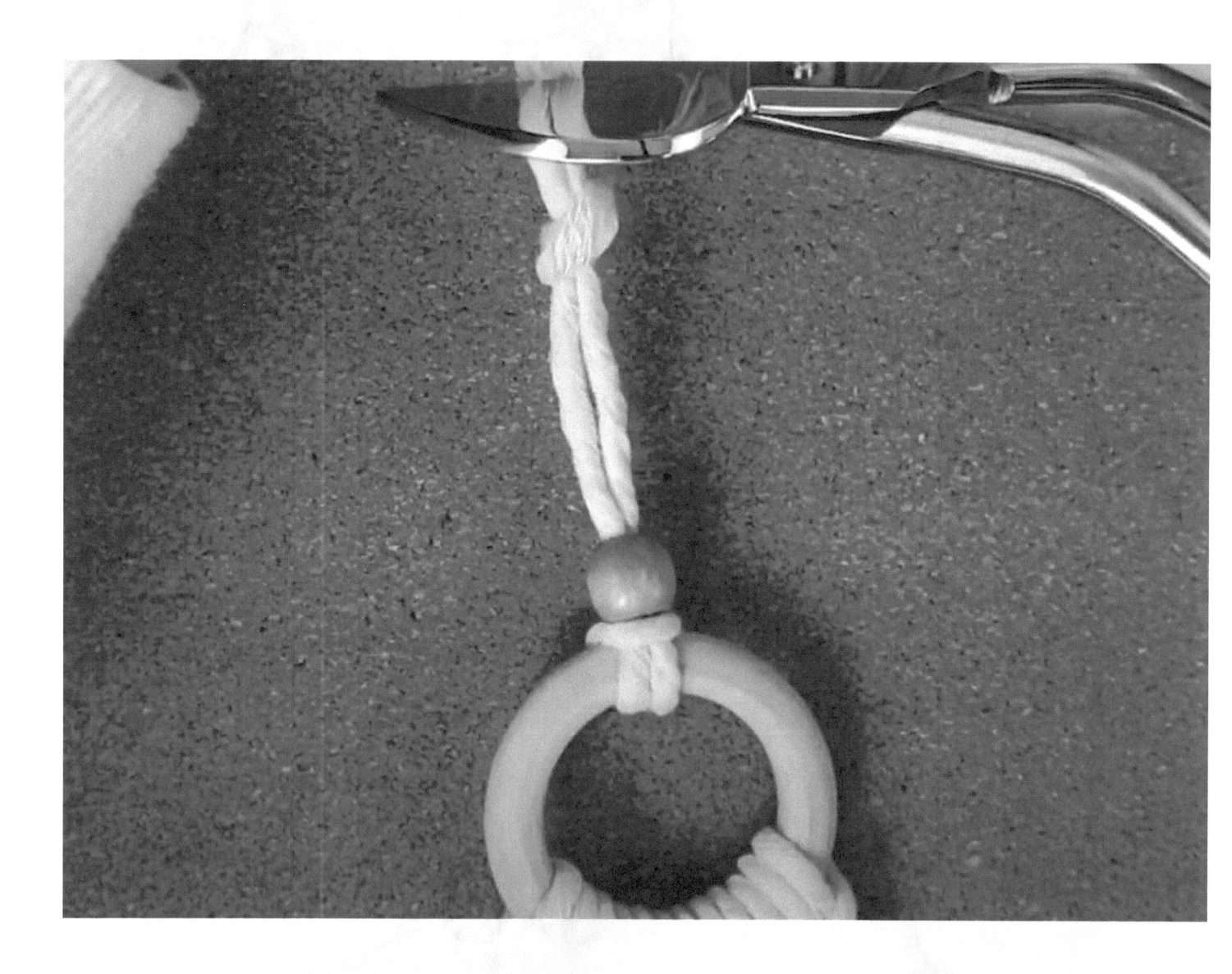

109

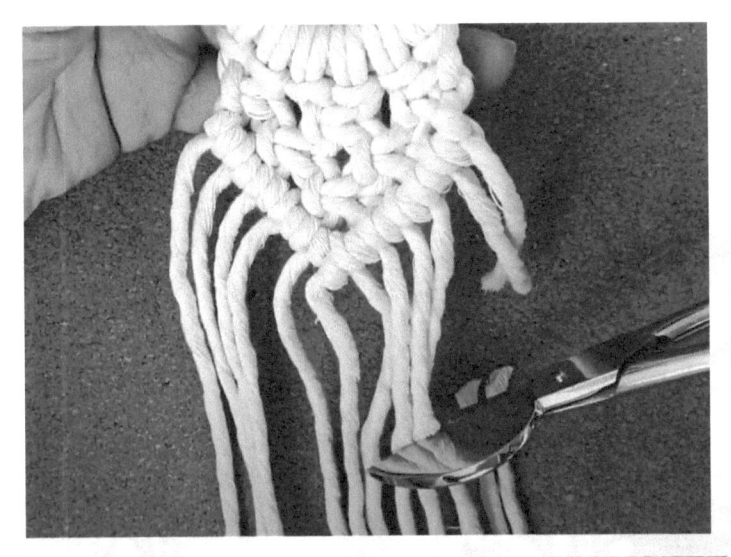

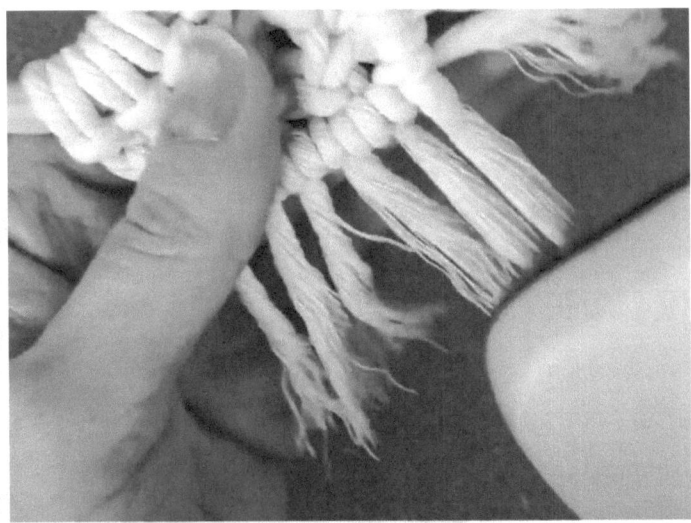

For Holydays

CHRISTMAS WREATH

Materials Required

- 4 mm 3-strand twisted green cotton (24 pieces @ 12" long)
- 3" metal ring
- 40" long sparkle yarn (I used Wool-Ease Thick and Quick)
- Twine for hanger
- Cork board or macramé board
- T-pins
- Sharp scissors

Photo Credits: (Marching North)

Instructions

Step 1

Attach all the green pieces of cord to the ring using lark's head knots. They should fill up the ring. If your ring is larger, you might need more pieces (or less if it's smaller).

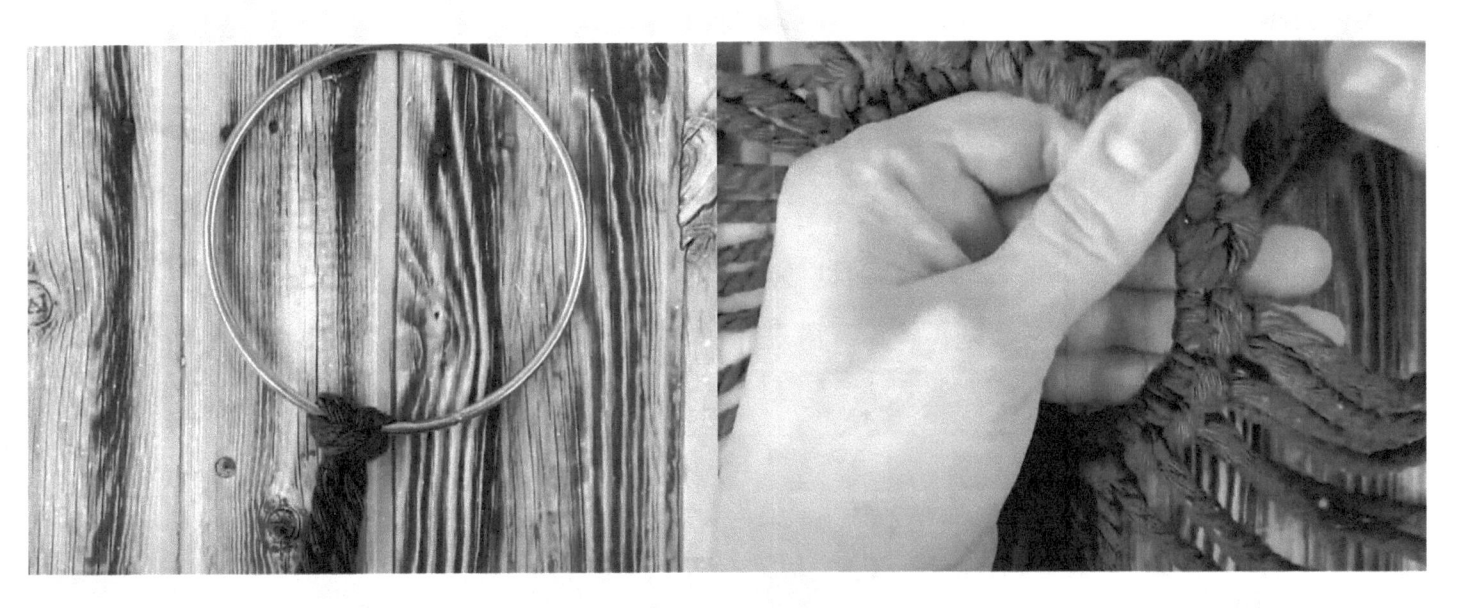

Photo Credits: (Marching North)

Step 2

Lay the piece of yarn around the ring. This is going to be the filler cord for a row of DHH knots going all the way around.

Starting at the bottom center, tie a DHH knot going to the right. This is what the first half will look like…

112

...and here's the second half.

Step 3

Continue tying double half hitch knots with each piece of cord going all the way around.

Once you get all the knots tied, pull on the filler cord ends to even them up a bit. We're going to tie a bow with them in minute.

Brush out the fringe all the way around.

Trim the fringe down as short as you want, I went with about 3/4" or so long.

Step 4

Tie a neat-looking bow with the ends of the filler cord yarn.

Grab a piece of twine and attach it with a lark's head knot to the metal ring at the top of the ornament. Just scoot the cord apart to make a little gap.

Then pull the ends up and behind the ornament so you can't see the hanger from the front.

Step 5

Grab a piece of twine and attach it with a lark's head knot to the metal ring at the top of the ornament. Just scoot the cord apart to make a little gap.

Then pull the ends up and behind the ornament so you can't see the hanger from the front.

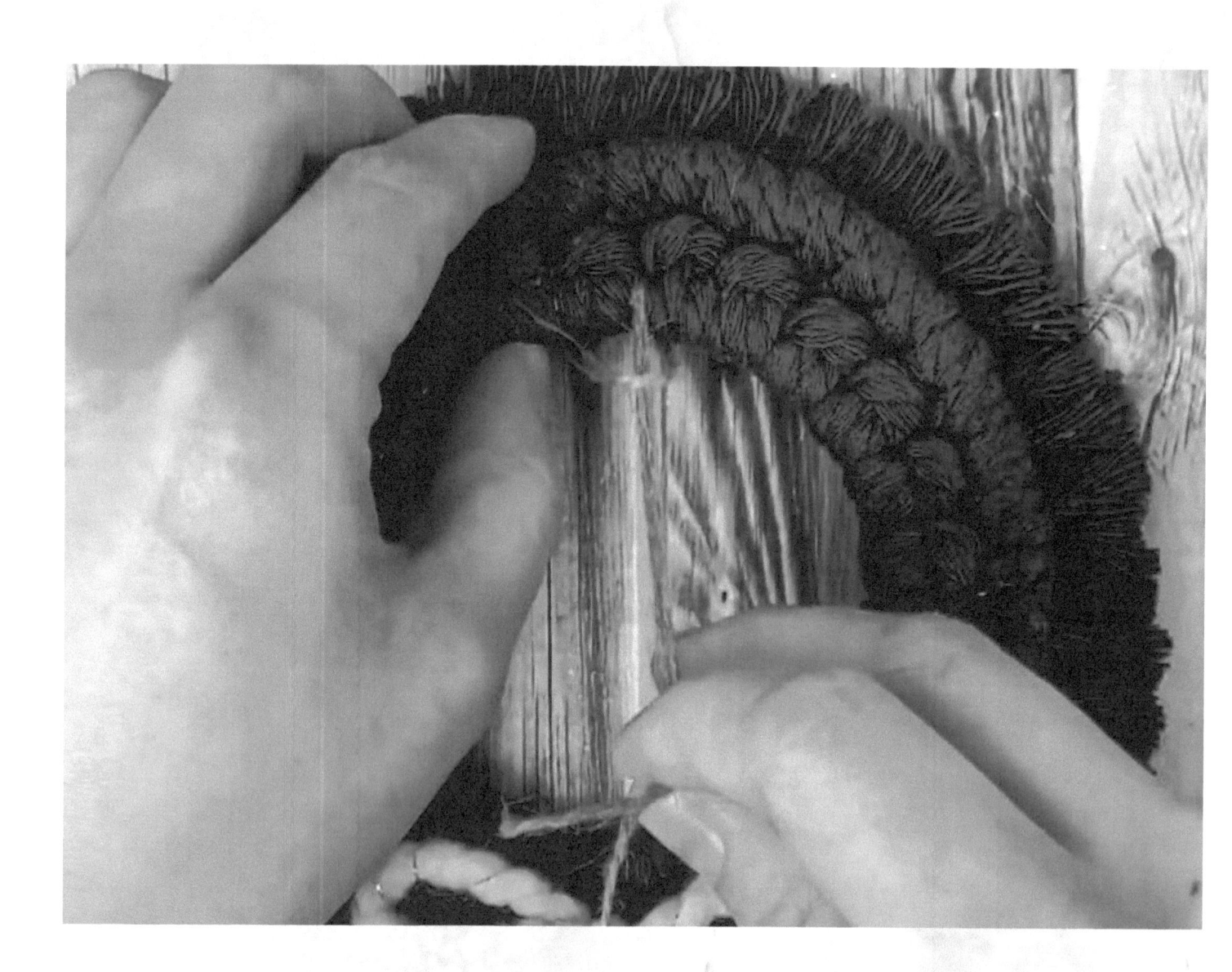

Tie an overhand knot in the end of the hanging loop and trim off the excess twine.

116

Christmas Wreath is Ready!

117

For Holydays

PUMPKIN COVER

Materials Required

- One Large Pumpkin
- 3mm Macramé Cord
- Scissors
- Measuring Tape

Instructions

Step 1 - Measure and Cut All Macramé Cord

First, measure all of your macramé cords.

Start by taking the end of the cord and wrapping it around the top of the pumpkin where you want the cover to sit when finished.

Measure that piece and fold it to double it.

Mine measured 14 inches so when I folded it I had 28 inches.

Set aside the cord we cut and continue measuring.

Now, to figure out how long to cut your cord, measure how far down the pumpkin you want the cover to hang.

Once you have done that, multiply that number by 8.

I wanted mine to hang 6 inches down, so I cut each macramé cord at 48 inches or 4 ft.

Ok, now that we have our measurements, on to cutting the cord!

Take the cord, measure the amount from before, in this case, 28 inches, add the 48 inches, and cut!

Set this piece aside as we will be using it in the next step.
Now, cut out 28 more pieces of 48-inch cords.

You should have a total of 29 cords cut going into the next step.

Step 2 - Create the Base For the Macramé Topper

Take the piece of cord that has the extra 28 inches on it and fold it in half.

Measure down 7 inches and cross the two cord tails over one another at the 7-inch line.

Now, take one piece of the 48 inch cord, fold it in half and slip the loop under the crossed section.

From here take the tails of this piece through the loop creating Lark's Head knot.

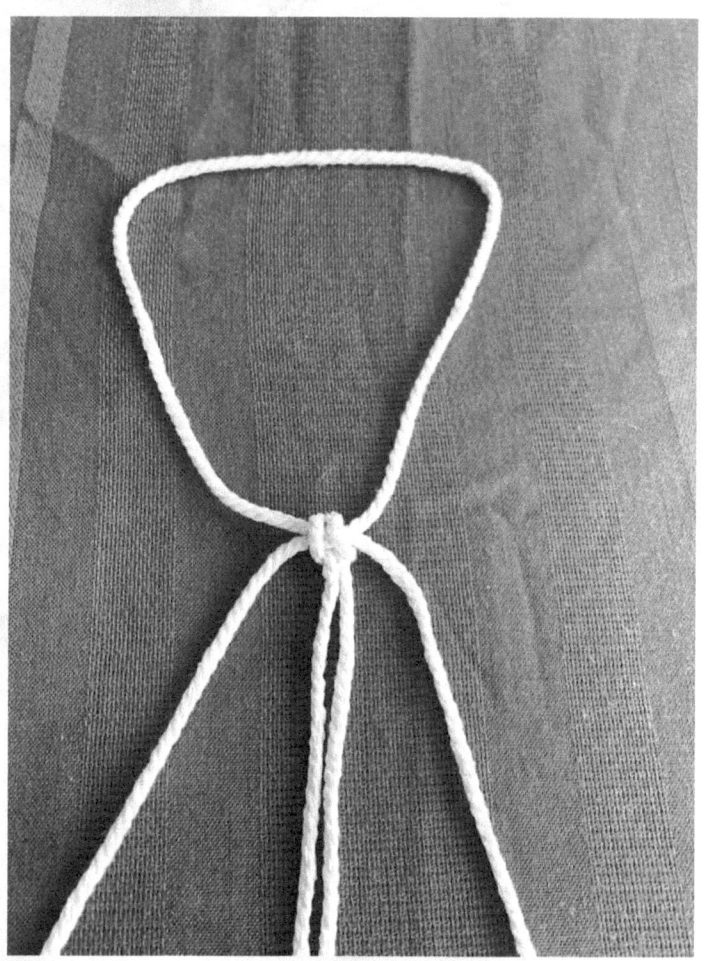

This will connect the pieces together, creating a circle to which we will now add our remaining cord.

Next, taking the right tail of the piece of cord that makes up the circle, create another larks head knot over the two pieces.

Repeat this on the left side and all the way around on both sides until you have one 48-inch chord left.

Make sure you keep wrapping the tails of the circle back around under the lark's head knots, keeping them even, as you will use these for the macramé pattern as well.

Now, once you have one piece left, similar to how you connected the circle together at the beginning, you will close off the circle.

Overlap the two tails of the circle, and over the crossed section put one more lark's head knot.

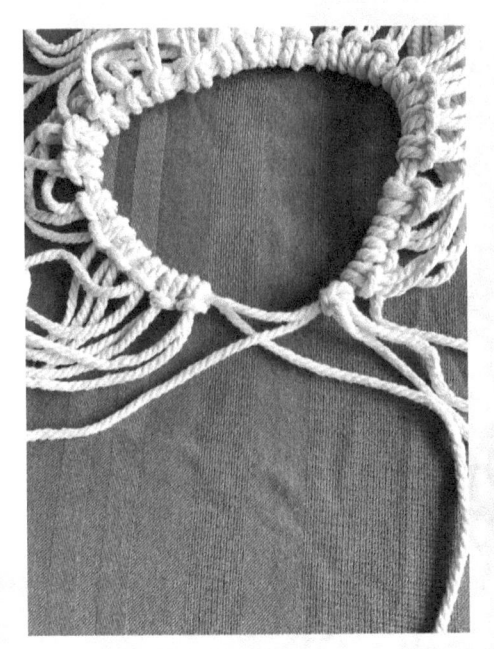

Step 3 - Create the Macramé Pattern

Now we are on to the fun part!

Start by putting the circle on the top of your pumpkin, we will be working our macramé here!

Separate all the cords into 5 sections of 12 strands of the cord. This will include the two tail chords from the circle. I started with those 4 cords from the closing to make sure they all stayed together and to keep the sections even.

It's easiest for me to count the closing section as two lark's head knots and then group each section together in 5 groups of 6 lark's head knots.

Now, starting with the group that has the closing section of 4 strands, create a triangle of square knots, going from 3 to 2, to 1.

Finish the triangle off with a line of double half-hitch (DDH) knots on either side.

Repeat this step in the rest of the sections.

Now, there will be a large gap between each triangle, we will be using cords from two triangles for this next step.

Starting from the middle gap, count in 4 cords from the middle on the right-hand side.

Grab the 4th cord as your holding cord and make a line of DDH knots towards the center of the gap, until you reach the first cord.

127

Repeat this step on the other side, creating a line of DHH, until you reach the middle of the gap.

Next, count 3 cords in from the middle gap, starting on the right-hand side again. Two inches down from the first DHH knots, create another line of DHH, stopping at the first in the middle as before.

Repeat on the other side, only this time connect the two together.

Trim off the extra cord, following the shape of the triangle, so you have about 1 inch of cord left.

Next, repeat the gap steps all the way around.

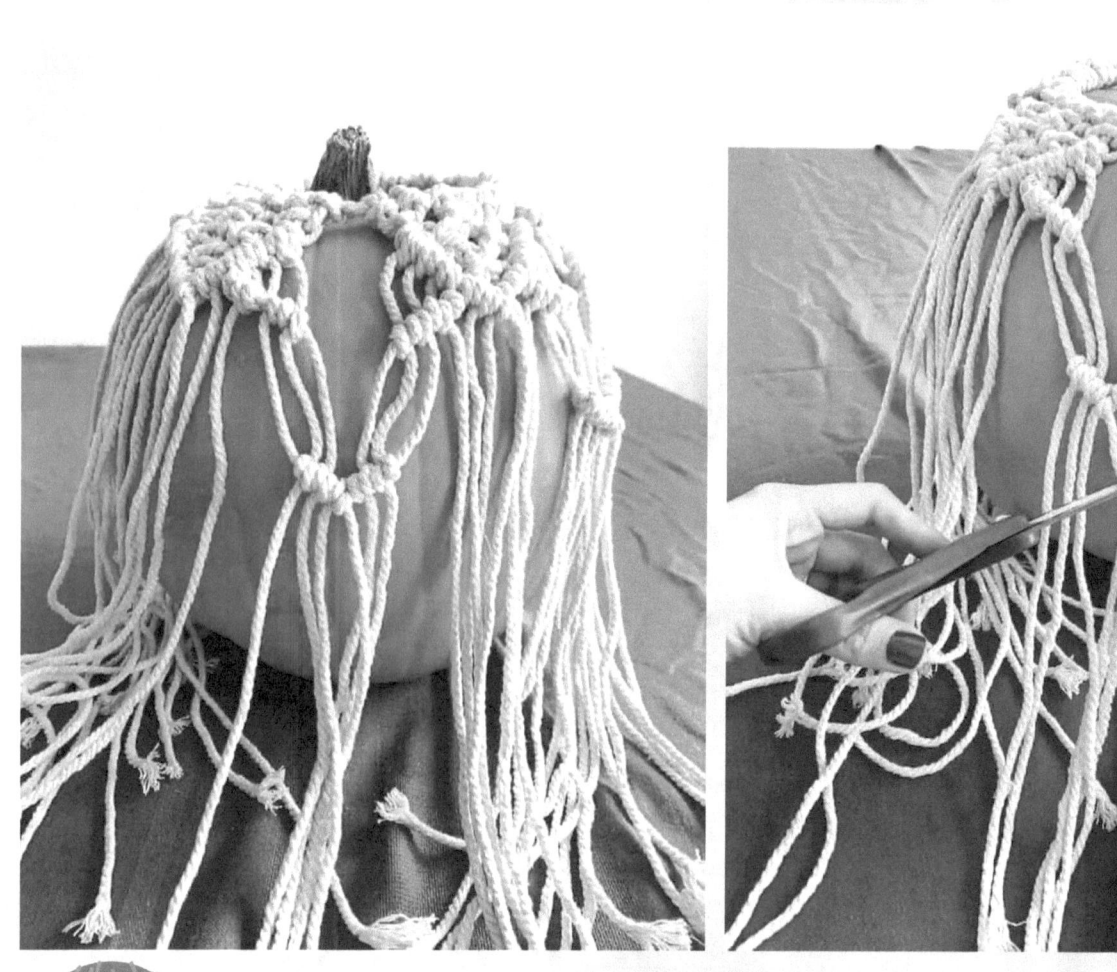

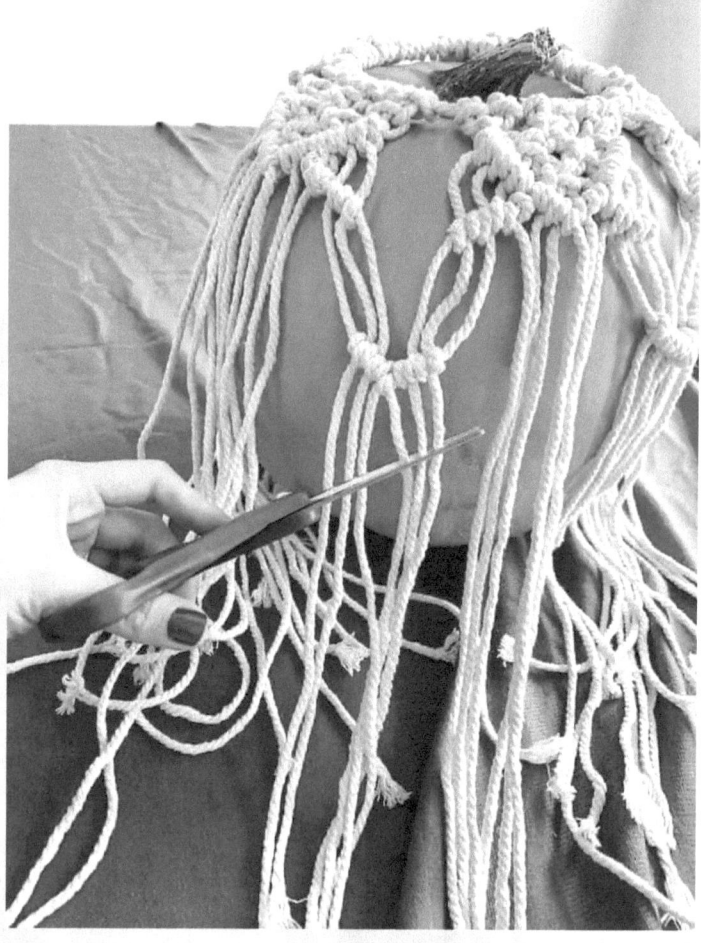

Now, with the remaining cord at the tip of the triangles, join it all together using a wrap knot.

Cut off the extra cord, leaving about 3 inches from the wrap. Repeat this step all the way around.

Now all that is left is to unravel all the remaining cord tails to create a nice boho fringe!

And there you have it, your own lovely macramé pumpkin cover!

SPOOKY

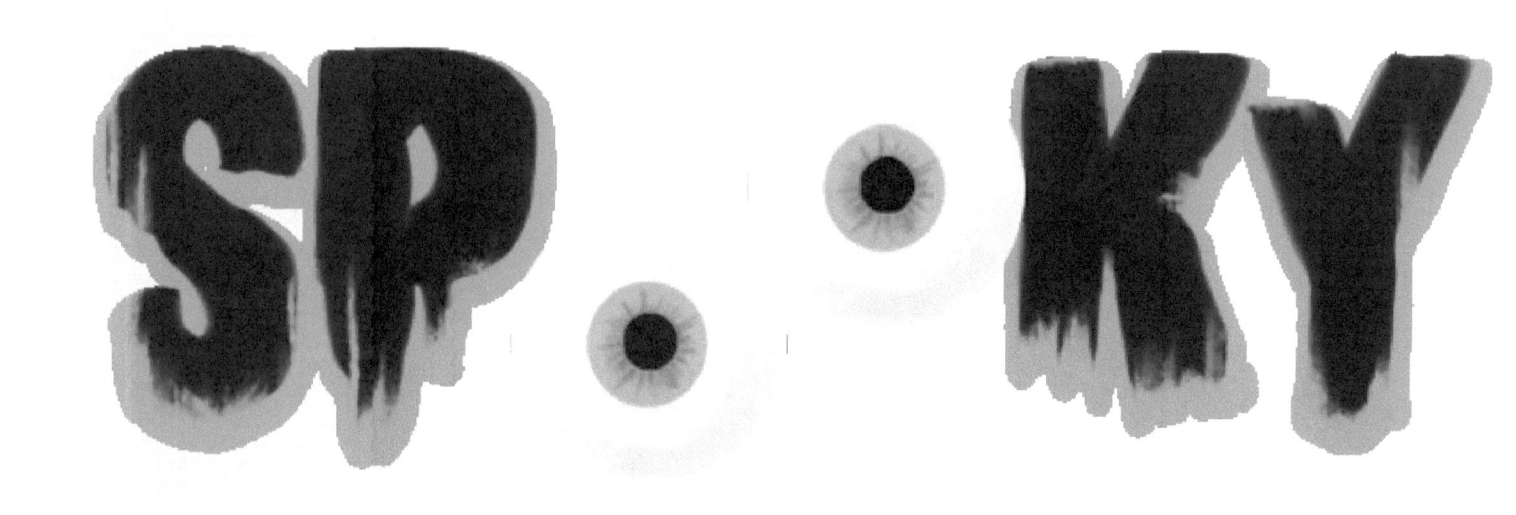

For Accessories

MASON JARS

Materials Required

- Macramé Cord
- Scissors
- Mason Jars

Instructions

Step 1 - Measure and Cut All Macramé Cord

For this project – I made two jars. One regular-sized mason jar and one larger sized mason jar with a handle.

I cut the cords all the same lengths for both jars – you will have to cut off some excess on the regular-sized jar at the end. But it's always better to have too much cord than too little.

You will need 6-SIX Foot cords for the larger jar, and 8-SIX Foot cords for the regular jar.

Step 2 - Attach Cording to the Jars

To begin each jar : Regular: Take two of your 6 ft cords and wrap them around the lip of the jar – secure them with a single square knot. Larger: Take one of your 6 ft cords and wrap them around the lip of the jar – secure with a regular knot.

Then, attach the rest of your cords to these cords. Regular: Take the rest of your 6 cords and attach them to your jar using reverse lark's head knots. Larger: Take the rest of your 5 cords and attach them to your jar using reverse lark's head knots. Evenly space the knots all around the lip of the jar.

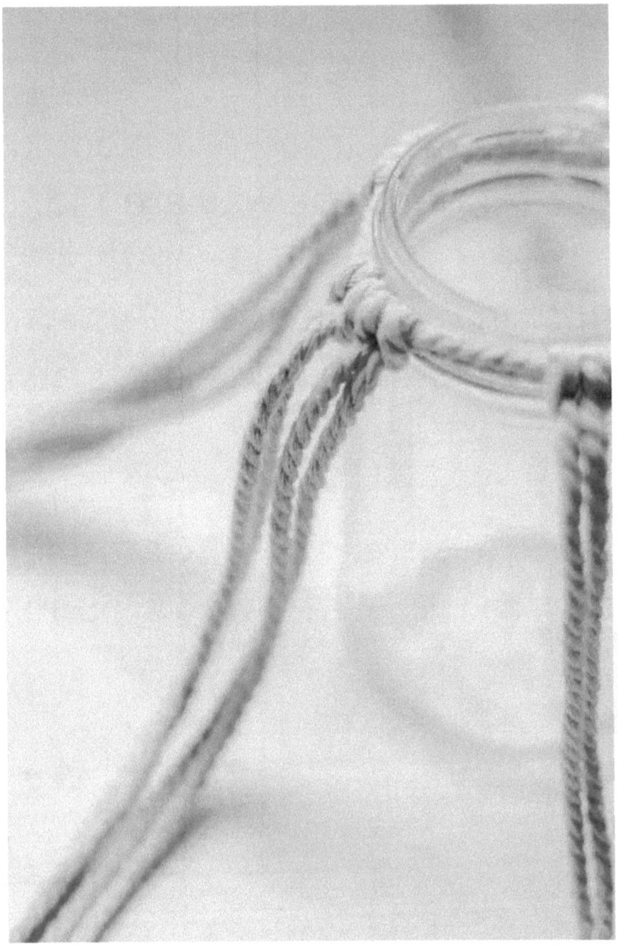
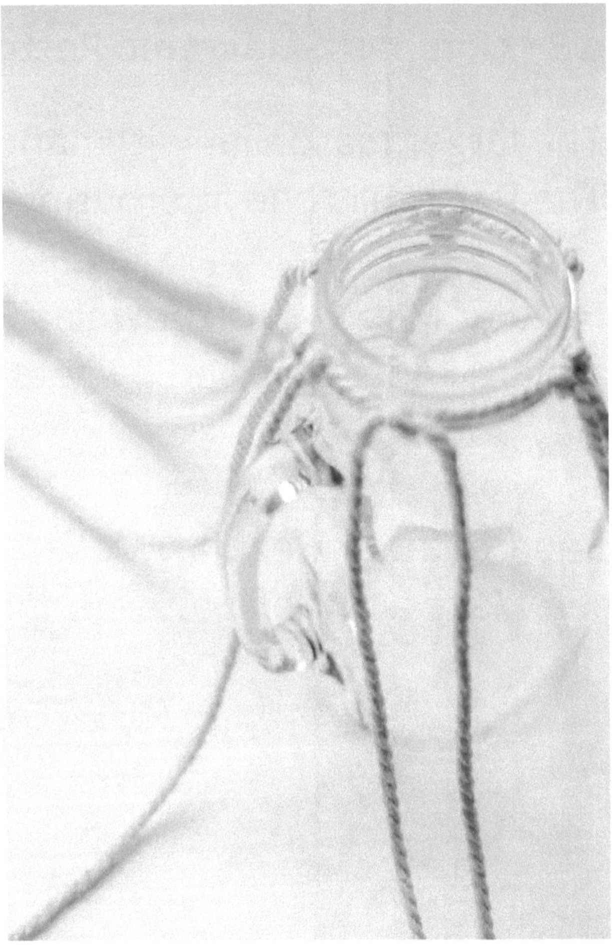
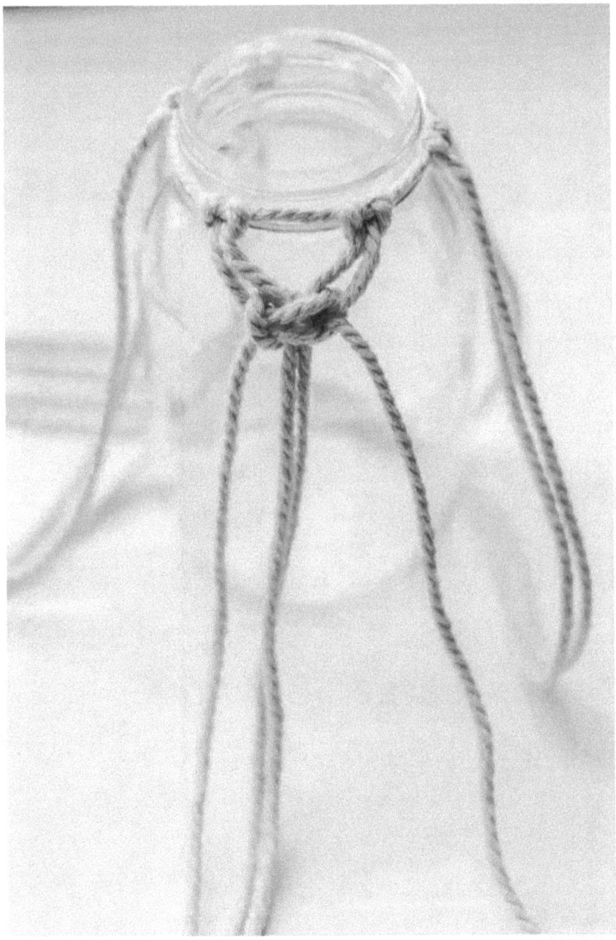
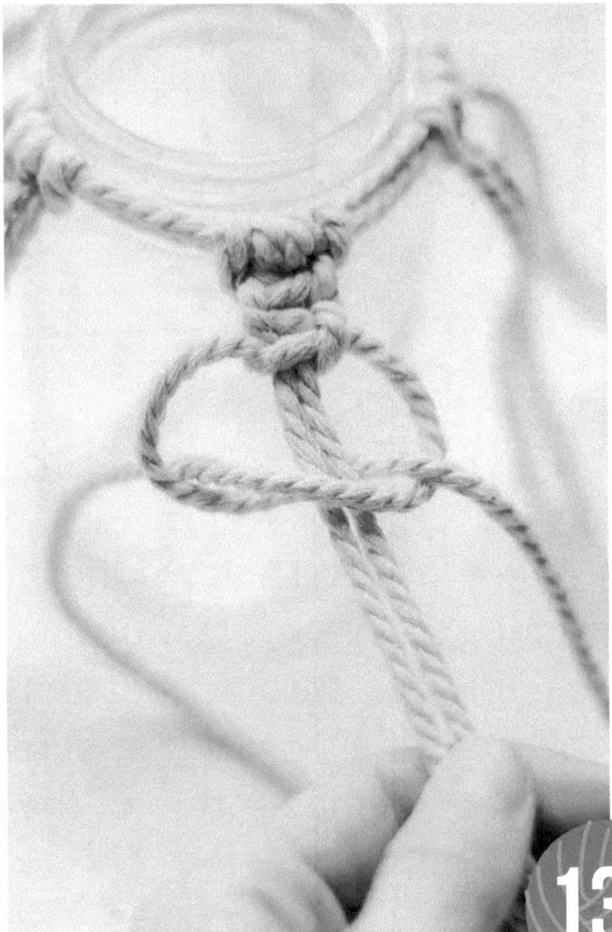

Step 3 - Complete Macramé Pattern

- The larger mason jar with handle (known as Larger in this book): The Pattern is one alternating square knot all the way around.

- Regular Mason Jar (known as Regular in this book): The Pattern is 2 square knots followed by sets of 2 alternating square knots all the way around.

Tie Square Knots: Regular: Make 2 square knots all the way around. Larger: Make a row of 1 alternating square knot all the way around the jar.

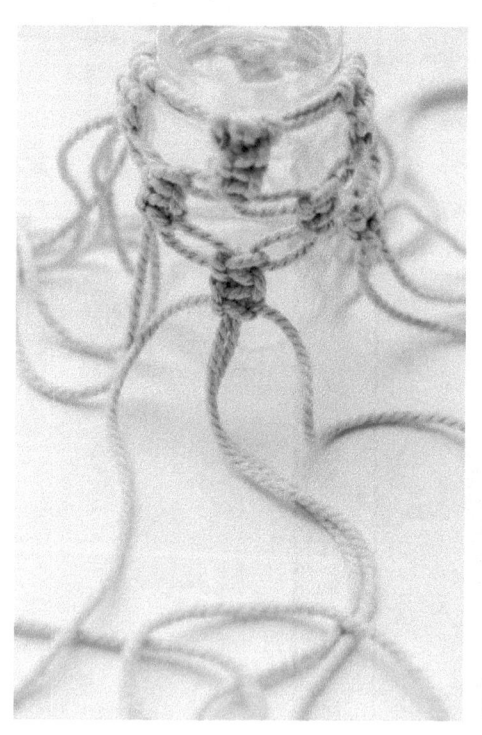

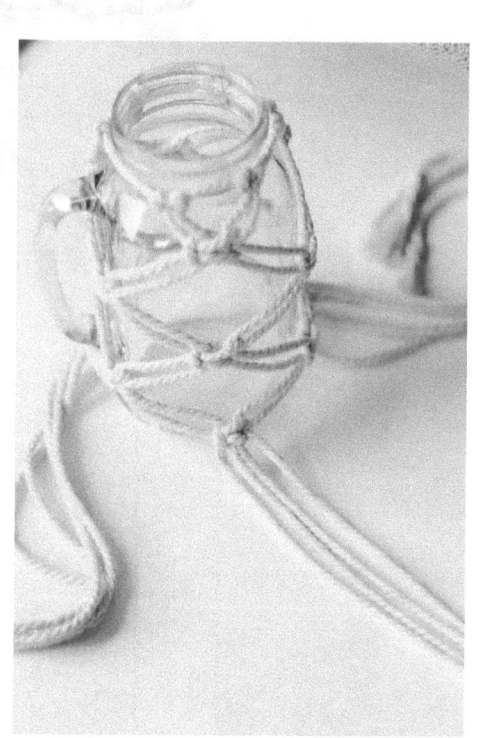

Continue the Pattern down the jar: Regular: Now make a row of 2 alternating square knots. Continue these rows of alternating square knots until you get to the bottom of the jar. Larger: Continue with another row of alternating square knots all the way around. Do this until you reach the bottom of the jar.

Step 4 - How to Finish the Jar

Finish the Jar: Regular/Larger: When you get to the bottom of the jar, cut off some excess rope but leave a bit there and comb them out for a fringe look.

That's it! How pretty do these look? I put some tea candles in my macramé mason jars for a nice glow!

For Accessories

MACRAMÉ PLACEMATS

Materials Required

- Cording
- Sharp Scissors
- Hanger

136

Instructions

1. Start by cutting 20 pieces of cords each 116 inches long. This part is tedious, I know. ●
2. Attach each of the 20 cords to your hanger using Lark's Head Knots.
3. Leave a space of about an 1.5 inches and from there make a row of square knots, followed by a row of alternating square knots.
4. Continue this pattern until you have 5 rows of square knots.
5. Take 8 adjacent cords, and tie a knot with the two cords in the center. Each of these "center" cords will be used as your leader cord. One center cord will be worked on the diagonal to the left, and the other to the right. We are making a diamond shape. Woot!
6. Take the center cord on the right and place it over the three cords to the right. Attach each of the three cords using double half hitch knots. Take the center cord on the left and place it over the three cords to the left. Attach each of these three cords using double half hitch knots. You should have a triangle shape when you are finished! Do you see it?
7. Now – take your leader cords and push them aside for a minute. You are going to make a square knot in the center of the triangle. Instead of having two middle cords, you will have four! (Watch the video above for a good view).
8. Continue making the bottom of the diamond shape by creating double half hitch knots but working it towards the middle.
9. Once your two rows of double half hitch knots meet in the middle, just tie a little knot. This helps tighten it together.
10. Now – we are back to making 5 rows of square knots!
11. Repeat the same pattern three times—>(5 rows of square knots, diamond with double half hitch and square knot in center)

12. Once you are finished with your pattern, cut your placemat off the hanger, just below the lark's head knots.

13. Hang your placemat evenly over your hanger or fold it in half. Trim the other side of the placemat so it's even with the first side you cut off.

For Accessories

MACRAMÉ BANNER

Materials Required

- Macramé Cording – 1 – 7 foot cord, and 40 – 3 feet cords.
- Beads (optional)
- Scissors
- Wire Brush (for fringe)

Instructions

1. Attach 8 of the three-foot cords to your long cord using Larks Head knots.
2. Make three rows of alternating square knots.
3. On the 4th row, make two square knots with the very inner cords.
4. On the 5th row, make one square knot with the 4 middle cords.
5. Make two rows on either side in a v shape of diagonal double half hitch knots. Follow the direction of your square knots above.
6. Make a tight square knot with the very center cords, bringing the V shape together.
7. Cut excess cords from the bottom and use a wire brush to fringe the ends.

For Accessories

MACRAMÉ GARLAND

Materials Required

- 3mm Macramé Cord
- Scissors
- Small Command Hooks (for hanging)

141

Instructions

1. Measure the length of the space you want to hang your garland in and cut a piece of cord at that length plus 8". (We cut ours at 80" for a 6' garland)
2. Tie loops at each end of this long cord and hang from your two command hooks.
3. Cut 54 cords (or twice the number of hanging knots you want on your garland) at 32" and attach them to your main cord using Lark's Head Knots.
4. Space the cords out in groups of 2 that are 2" apart.
5. Tie each group of 2 cords into a Berry Knot.
6. Trim the tails to varying (or uniform, if you prefer) lengths and fray the ends of the cords.

Turn this Hobby into Side Hustle

Turn this Hobby into Side Hustle

If you're looking for a way to make some extra money, you may want to consider macramé. Not only is macramé relatively easy to learn, but it's also a very popular craft right now. This means that there's a good market for selling macramé items. In this blog chapter, I'll give you some tips on how to make money from it as a side hustle. So if you're ready to start earning some extra cash, read on!

SELL YOUR MACRAMÉ PIECES TO FRIENDS AND FAMILY

One of the best ways to make money from macramé is to sell your pieces to friends and family. This can be a great way to get started, as you will likely have a built-in market of people who are interested in your work. Plus, selling to people you know can be a great way to build up your reputation as an artist.

There are a few things to keep in mind when selling to friends and family: (next page)

SET A FAIR PRICE FOR YOUR WORK

Don't undervalue your pieces just because they are going to people you know. At the same time, don't overcharge them either. Come up with a fair price that reflects the time and effort you put into each piece.

SELL TO INTERESTED CUSTOMERS

Make sure the person you are selling to is actually interested in buying macramé art. There's no point in trying to sell something to someone who has no interest in it.

BE PREPARED TO ANSWER QUESTIONS ABOUT YOUR WORK

People who are interested in buying macramé from you will likely have questions about the process, materials, etc. Be prepared to answer these questions so that they feel confident in their purchase.

SELL YOUR MACRAMÉ PIECES AT LOCAL CRAFT FAIRS

If you're looking for a way to make some extra money, why not try your hand at macramé? Macramé is a fun and easy craft that anyone can learn, and it's a great way to add a personal touch to your home decor.

One of the best ways to sell your macramé pieces is to participate in local craft fairs. This gives you the opportunity to meet potential customers face-to-face and show off your work. You can also use this time to chat with other crafters and get ideas for new projects.

To get started, simply create a list of the fairs in your area that you'd like to participate in. Then, start creating some beautiful pieces! Remember to take pictures of your work so you can promote it online. And once you start selling, don't forget to spread the word about your new side hustle.

BECOME A LOCAL WHOLESALER

As a local wholesaler, you can sell macramé products to stores in your area. This is a great way to get started in the macramé business because it doesn't require a lot of start-up capital. You can find wholesale suppliers online or at craft fairs.

To be successful as a local wholesaler, you need to build good relationships with store owners and buyers. You also need to offer competitive prices and create quality products.

GIVE LOCAL WORKSHOPS

If you're interested in making money from macramé as a side hustle, one option is to give local workshops. This can be a great way to share your passion for macramé while also earning some extra income.

When planning your workshop, be sure to consider the needs of your audience. What level of experience do they have? What are their goals for taking the workshop? Once you have a good understanding of your audience, you can start planning the content of your workshop.

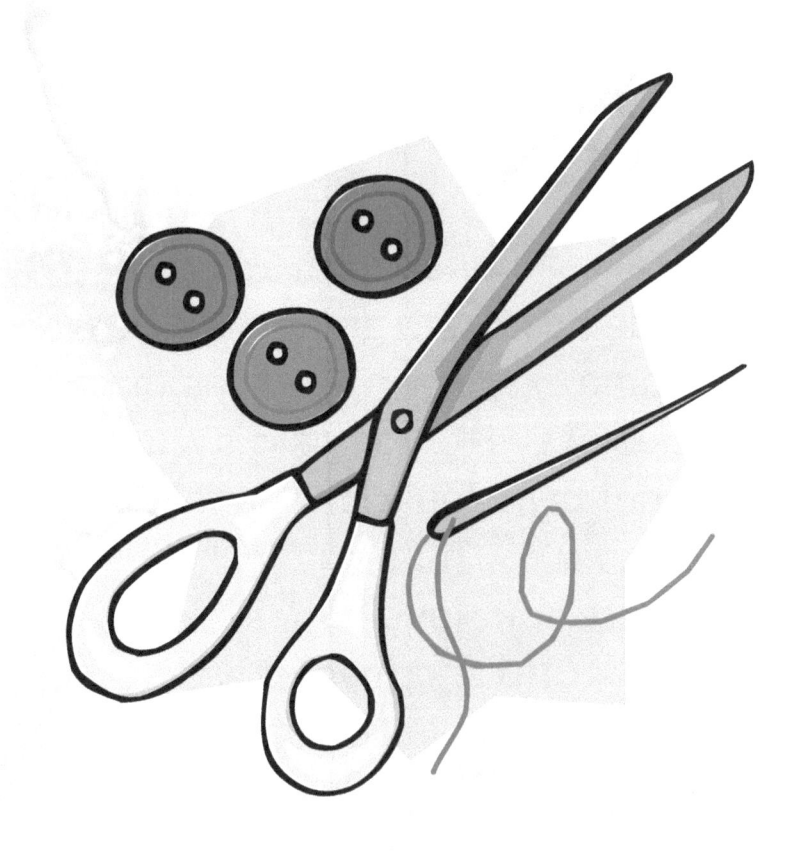

Some things to keep in mind as you plan:

-What types of knots will you teach?

-How will you structure the class? Will it be demonstration-based, or will participants be working on their own projects?

-What kind of materials will you need, and how much will they cost?

-What kinds of project ideas will you share with participants?

By thinking through these questions ahead of time, you'll be able to create a workshop that's enjoyable and informative for everyone involved.

START A YOUTUBE CHANNEL

Making money from Macramé as a side hustle is a great way to earn some extra cash. And one of the best ways to do this is by starting your own YouTube channel.
With a YouTube channel, you can share your love for Macramé with the world and reach a wider audience than you ever could have imagined. Plus, you can make money from ads and sponsorships, and even sell your own products through your channel.

But before you can start earning money from your YouTube channel, there are a few things you need to do first. Here's a quick guide on how to start a successful YouTube channel for your Macramé business: (Next Page)

FIND YOUR NICHE

The first step to starting a successful YouTube channel is finding your niche. What kind of Macramé videos do you want to make? There are endless possibilities, but it's important to narrow down your focus so that you can build an audience that's interested in what you have to offer.

Some ideas for Macramé niche channels include:

-Macramé tutorials
-Macramé product reviews
-Macramé inspiration videos
-How-to videos for specific Macramé techniques
-Macramé vlogs (video logs) documenting your journey as a macramist

CREATE ENGAGING CONTENT

Once you know what kind of content you want to create, it's time to start filming!

And before you start to record the video make sure to have your script or table of content ready for you so that you don't miss anything. A script is helpful in making a video more engaging because sometimes when you are going to make the video, you put energy into giving information and forget to say something that can keep the readers watching you till the end. Also, try to add some humor into the videos, don't be boring because people have a short time span for focus now-a-days.

SELL YOUR MACRAMÉ PIECES ONLINE

As a macramé artist, you can sell your pieces online through a number of different platforms. Etsy is a popular option for handmade goods, and you can also sell through your own website or blog. Social media platforms like Instagram and Facebook are also great ways to reach potential customers.

To get started, create a portfolio of your work to showcase to potential buyers. Take high-quality photos of your pieces, and write detailed descriptions that include the materials used and the dimensions of each piece. When you list your items for sale, be sure to set realistic prices that reflect the time and effort you put into each one.

Promote your work regularly on social media, and consider running ads on platforms like Etsy or Google Adwords. You can also participate in craft fairs or pop-up shops to get exposure for your business. With some hard work and dedication, you can build a successful side hustle selling macramé artwork online!

BECOME AN ONLINE CORD STOCKIST

As someone who loves to craft, you may have considered turning your hobby into a side hustle. And what better way to do that than by becoming an online cord stockist?

There are a few things you need to know before getting started, like what type of cord to buy and how to price your products. But don't worry, we've got you covered with all the information you need to get started selling macramé cord online.

WHERE TO BUY MACRAMÉ CORD

There are a few different places you can buy macramé cord online, but our favorite is Amazon. They have a great selection of cords at different prices, so you can find something that fits your budget. Plus, they offer free shipping on orders over $25, which is always a bonus.

HOW TO PRICE YOUR PRODUCTS

quality cord that's durable and in high demand, you can lean towards the higher end of the pricing spectrum, around $1 per foot. On the other hand, if you're using a more basic cord or targeting a price-sensitive market, you might opt for the lower end of the range, around $0.50 per foot.

However, pricing isn't solely about covering your material costs; you also need to consider other factors like labor, overhead, and desired profit margins. Here are some additional steps to help you determine a fair and profitable price for your cord-based products:

Calculate Material Costs: Determine how much cord, along with any additional materials like clasps or beads, is used in each product. This is your base material cost per item.
Factor in Labor Costs: Consider the time it takes to create each product. Calculate how many items you can produce in an hour and multiply that by your desired hourly wage. Add this labor cost to your material cost.
Overhead Costs: Include any overhead expenses related to your business, such as rent, utilities, marketing, and packaging. Divide these costs by the number of products you expect to sell to allocate a portion of overhead to each item.
Profit Margin: Decide on the profit margin you want to achieve. This is typically a percentage of your total costs (material, labor, and overhead). For instance, if you want a 30% profit margin, add 30% of your total costs to the cost calculation.
Competitive Analysis: Research your competitors' prices to ensure your pricing is in line with the market. If your products offer unique features or higher quality, you may be able to charge a premium.

Testing and Adjusting: Start with your calculated price, but be prepared to adjust based on customer feedback and sales data. It's important to strike a balance between being competitive and ensuring you're making a profit.

Consider Value-Added Services: If you offer customization, special packaging, or exceptional customer service, you can justify higher prices. Highlight these value-added services to justify a premium.

Promotions and Discounts: Plan for occasional promotions or discounts to attract new customers or encourage repeat business. Ensure that your regular prices still cover your costs and profit goals.

Monitor and Adapt: Keep an eye on market trends, material cost fluctuations, and changes in customer preferences. Adjust your pricing strategy accordingly to remain competitive and profitable.

In conclusion, pricing your cord-based products involves a combination of cost analysis, market research, and business strategy. By considering all relevant factors and regularly reviewing your pricing strategy, you can set prices that not only cover your expenses but also generate a healthy profit for your business while meeting customer expectations.

Scan the QR Code to receive over 30 macramé patterns for free

Made in United States
Troutdale, OR
11/18/2023